Believe It or Not

Mama Likes the Nursing Home!

Kathryn Martin

Ella,

Keep smiling.

Kathryn Martin

Beacon Hill Press of Kansas City
Kansas City, Missouri

ISBN 083-411-6189

Printed in the
United States of America

Cover design: Ted Ferguson
Cover illustration: Keith Alexander

All Scripture quotations are from the King James Version.

Library of Congress Cataloging-in-Publication Data
Martin, Kathryn
    Believe it or not—Mama likes the nursing home / Kathryn Martin.
    p. cm.
  ISBN 0-8341-1618-9 (pbk.)
    1. Aging parents—Care—United States.   2. Life change events—
United States.   3. Adjustment (Psychology) in old age.   4. Nursing
homes—Sociological aspects.   5. Nursing homes—Psychological as-
pects.   I. Title.
HQ1064.U5M383   1996
306.874'3—dc20   96-2628
                                                                      CIP

10   9   8   7   6   5   4   3   2

CONTENTS

FOREWORD

Each day thousands of people grapple with the difficult decision of whether or not a nursing home is a solution to their problems. Sometimes elderly people realize their needs when they are no longer able to care for themselves properly. More often it is a son or a daughter who must decide that a nursing home is the only answer.

As much as adult children love their mother or father, they may not be in a position to receive the parent into their homes to provide the needed care. They may be physically incapable. They may already have a sick spouse or handicapped child to care for. In most cases, they cannot afford to hire outside help. As much as they would like to be with the parents and care for them personally, often there seems no way to do it.

Kathryn Martin faced that problem. And later her mother, Cecil Martin, made her own decision to reenter a nursing home.

In this book, Kathryn, known across the United States and Canada as an inspirational speaker and as country humorist Miz Maudie, tells the story of her mother's true experiences as a nursing home resident. It begins with the story of one woman's acceptance of the end of her life. But it continues as the story of courage, pathos, and humor when in determining to glean the good from her last days, she finds instead the beginning of a new life.

—Jacklyn Welch Shockley

ACKNOWLEDGMENTS

My heart overflows with immeasurable gratitude and appreciation for the many people who have touched our lives, bringing hope, health, and happiness to Mother and me.

It would take a second book much bigger than this one to list all of you. But in the limited space allotted I wish to thank—

Shona Fisher, who proves an editor can have heart;

Jacklyn Welch Shockley, my mentor and second mother, who has so patiently listened, advised, and encouraged throughout the experiences and the writing;

Dr. Edmund and Susan Spiller and Dr. Michael Kozel; nursing staff Madee Edwards, Georgette Anderson, Debra Lewis, Mary Lou Pierson Burris, and Lena Graziano; social services staff Shirley Gabriel, Terry Voight, Sandi Daniels, Marie Troyer, and Rita Jones; nursing home personnel Jo Ann Hollie, Ann Scallan, Sandra Tanner, Evelyn Williams, Ola Mae Pea, Gwen Tobey, Diane "Rhode Island" Addison, Ann Carter, Gloria Johnson, Dwight Franklin, Brad Davis, Laura Cousain, Dorothy McDonald, Maxine Windham, Sandy O'Neal, Dorothy Alexander, Tidy Batiste, Stephanie Sparks, "Red" Guitreau, Paul Guitreau (administrator), Emma Pines, Gail Pines, Virginia Henry, Willie Mae Carter, Elaine Varnado, Michelle Perkins, Mattie Perry, Ruth Morris, Cynthia Middlebrook, Virginia Jackson, and the aide who called Mama "Fish Fry" (wherever you are);

Mother's godchild, Barbara Ann Sterken Alack, and "grandson" Raymond Drude;

The nursing home residents who have become family, Doris Guess, Myrtle Owens, Dot Triplett, Elsie Nix, Hattie

Rudd, Eulah McGinnis, Carolyn Sullivan, Alberta Vanacore;

Our friends and relatives who have visited, written, or called so faithfully all this time;

My teachers, Audrey Bodker, Peggy King Jacob, Mary Alford Kinchen, Joyce Paul Perrin, and A. J. Bodker, who have stayed in closest contact through the years, always believing in me;

The memory of my father, Fernard Victor Martin, whose biggest dream was for his little girl to get the formal education he was denied (I have, Daddy);

My mother, Cecil Mae Price Martin, known for saying, "I'm a Kentuckian, and the words 'I can't' are not in my vocabulary";

Mr. B., who helped add to Mother's new life;

To those above and in the book, as well as the many others too numerous to name—

May God bless you as He has blessed me with you.

—Kathryn J. Martin

1

The Start of It All

IT WAS LATE AFTERNOON when the elevator doors opened and a hospital gurney was wheeled out. From it, Mother's cries echoed down the corridors.

"Ohhhh," she moaned and prayed. "Ohhhh Lord, help me!"

It was hard to recognize this groaning woman as the same one who had walked in on her own the day before and waved cheerfully on the way to back surgery that morning. Now Mother begged for mercy as she was placed into her bed.

"She's had a little something for pain, so she'll soon settle down," a nurse explained, adding, "She's not hurting as bad as she thinks she is."

She *didn't* settle down, and the long minutes turned into long hours. Proud of her strength to face anything, Mother had never carried on like this. So I knew she'd met her match, and that this unbearable pain was real.

I tried to comfort her, but she couldn't stand to be touched. I prayed softly with her. I quoted Scripture. I hummed some of her favorite hymns. I tried silence. She didn't seem aware of anything except the pain.

"My legs! Oh, my legs hurt so bad! Oh, Kathryn Joyce, Honey, do something!"

She went from whimpers to yelps and back again. Medication wasn't helping. Between moans and sudden jumps from restless naps, she seldom stopped talking.

"Ohhh, I hurt! My legs!" followed by "Did you remember to turn the lights out at the house? Oh, I'm adyin'! Honey, you don't have to stay with me. Go on home and get some rest. Ohhh!"

This surely didn't sound like my mother, who as a teenage teacher had faced down bullies in her one-room Kentucky schoolhouse, in her 30s had eloped just to prove she could keep a secret, in her 40s had challenged an intruder in the dark of night, and in her 70s had refused help and painted her entire house alone!

How I wished I'd never let her talk me into signing the papers for this surgery!

*   *   *

Physically Mother's appearance changed rapidly while the days and nights passed so slowly. Her long frame shortened by several inches, and her weight dropped from 175 pounds to less than 100. Yet, because of her helplessness, it took three strong professionals to lift or turn her.

I tried everything to tempt her to eat. I begged. I bribed. I fussed. I even tried to play "make the train go into the tunnel."

"Honey, I hurt so bad I can't eat. I don't want to eat. Ohhhh! I appreciate you trying to help me, but—ohhhh!" she would cry out again and again.

Her total daily intake consisted of a diuretic tablet, a few teaspoons of food, and drops of water. She was in diapers. Her long silver hair seemed to thin overnight, and I had to work at collecting enough to braid it into one little pigtail as she tossed her head from side to side in pain.

Visiting friends who saw the bony little body thought they'd entered the wrong room and apologized: "I'm sorry. I was looking for Mrs. Martin."

Some wondered why I was sitting with *this* patient while my own mother needed me. They fought to hide expressions of shock when I assured them, "This *is* Mama."

Yet no matter how weak she became, if she heard them, she always recognized and called each one by name.

She seldom stopped talking, usually asking questions—the same questions again and again—and demanding answers. At night the horrible pain worsened, and she hallucinated, annoyed because I couldn't clean the spots off the wall or let out the butterflies.

After so many days, nurses told me the doctor wanted to discharge her, since her medicare time would soon be up. He told me the nurses thought Mother was ready to go home, that she was "putting on."

Very courteously, I described past illnesses as I'd done before and explained that for Mother this equaled a sort of comatose state.

"She's in fine health," the doctor said curtly. "She should be on her way home. The surgery was a success. As soon as she gets stronger and takes a little physical therapy, she needs to get out of here."

When he left, I heard Mother moan, "Puttin' on! I'd like to see—ohhh—how much puttin' on—ohhh—he'd think it was—ohhh—if *he* was hurtin' like this—ohhhh."

Once again I wept silently, not knowing help was coming.

The next day her doctor was out of town, and the physician on duty came in right at the time Mother was the most incoherent, crying her usual, "Ohhhhhh, my legs, my legs—ohhh. What's that moving on the wall over—ohhhh, my legs." Her thrashing was weak but still obvious.

The doctor's eyes widened with concern. "How long has your mother been like this?" he asked.

"Since she came out of recovery after surgery," I answered. I felt exhilaration through my distress. Finally someone was going to listen to me!

"Let's get some blood work *stat!*" he ordered quietly but authoritatively. His words worked magic.

In a few minutes medical laboratory personnel arrived. Technicians and nurses scurried around. Blood samples were drawn. And that very night some answers were on the way.

"I wish I'd seen her in this condition sooner," the young, blond doctor told me. "The few mornings I've seen her she's appeared coherent and answered me."

"She's always been able to do that, Doctor," I answered. "Mother doesn't fall into deep unconsciousness the way most people do. She talks. She recognizes people. She gives the correct answers to questions. Yet later she doesn't remember much about even having been in the hospital."

I was almost limp from exhaustion and relief.

The lab report was delivered to the doctor, and it was just what he suspected. Because Mother had been in a lot of pain before her hospitalization, she had already lost much of her appetite but had continued the diuretic tablet. Now with the desire for food completely gone, she was still faithfully swallowing the fluid pill brought each day. Her body was losing vital chemicals, especially potassium. In fact, her potassium level was almost nonexistent. The terrible leg pain caused the doctor to suspect this condition.

Potassium treatments were begun immediately—and, unbelievably, by the next morning there were visible signs of a turn for the better. Mother fell into her first restful sleep in months.

But the weeks of potassium depletion had been cruel to their victim. She was so weak she couldn't hold a pen or even a spoon and didn't know what to do with either one. However, there was slight improvement, and the time had come to leave the hospital. But that wasn't as easy as I thought it would be.

2

But It Sounded So Simple

A FEW DAYS AFTER THE NEW TREATMENT BEGAN, the regular physician called me out into the hall.

"I'm prepared to discharge your mother any time now. However," he added so casually it didn't soak in, "she won't be able to care for herself anymore, so I'll release her *only* to a nursing home of your choosing."

I had wondered how I was going to manage, but in my tired, befuddled mind, I honestly thought this illness would be like all the others I'd nursed Mother through since my childhood. Always before, Mother became unbelievably ill, only to start mending, regain her strength, and soon be her usual happy, independent self.

"Oh, I'll take care of her," I answered. "I can stay for the next month."

I had that much time, because only two weeks before the surgery I had resigned as a college professor near Nashville and moved to Memphis. There a church had created a staff position especially for me that would enable me to make the transition to becoming a full-time speaker. I was to work with them when I was in town, gaining both experience and income, yet accept invitations to speak elsewhere until I was better known and my calendar of engagements filled.

The fatigue that overcame me after the relentless postsurgery hours was such that I really couldn't absorb the facts. It still took two people to turn Mother and three to lift her from the bed. And that was only a small part of tending her needs.

"You're not hearing me," the doctor repeated more emphatically. "Your mother will *never* be able to care for herself again. *You* won't be able to do it. The only way I'll release her is to a nursing care facility. Now you decide where you want to put her, and I'll help you in any way I can. I'll send social services here to talk with you. You need to get started."

I wish I had known about social services all along, for they are trained in this area. They know where, when, why, and whom to call. If I could have utilized their expertise, it would have saved me unbelievable amounts of time, money, miles, and effort.

However, in this case they were limited, because the hospital was located in a different parish (equivalent of a county) from Mama's home, and they could not work directly with main offices in our home parish. But they were kind and offered sufficient advice to tell me the usual procedures:

1. Go to Mother's parish seat and meet directly with a social services representative.
2. Select a nursing home and meet with its social services personnel.
3. Find a physician who could be depended on to visit the nursing home regularly and respond in an emergency.
4. Get a signature of release from the attending physician.
5. Arrange ambulance transportation from the hospital to the nursing home.

It all seemed so simple, so 1-2-3-4-5. Was I ever in for some surprises!

*   *   *

I settled Mother in for her morning nap and made the long drive to our parish's social services office. The woman assigned to our case realized my state of mind and discomfort at applying for assistance for the first time in our lives. By now, Mother's small savings as well as my own were spent. Part of my savings had been to live on in case I wasn't discovered as a speaker right away after leaving the college with its excellent salary and benefits.

Had I known about social services earlier, I would have been advised that I was not personally responsible for Mother's medical expenses and that she qualified for benefits from our own tax dollars. Not knowing this, I paid bill after bill, starting with those that required payment at the time of service. I had filled out medicare and personal insurance forms until I felt like screaming. Often the replies were rejections of part or all of the charges. So I paid those balances as well when they came due. I didn't know that I could have resubmitted claims and sometimes the second go-round brought a more fair assessment of charges.

For some billing departments it was probably standard procedure to stamp in red ink on a first statement, "Payable Immediately. Will Be Released to Collection Agency Within 10 Days." But to me, always avoiding debt and not used to bills, it served its purpose. Not knowing it was often a scare technique, I hurriedly paid. Better broke than to have Mother get well and discover her good credit with a smudge on it!

I filled out numerous forms at social services, but to complete them, I had to drive back to the social security office in one town and the bank in another for further information. Since Mama was a widow of a railroad employee, the Railroad Retirement Board as well as the social security office had to be given a nursing home address for future checks, and the bank needed that address for any direct-deposit checks that would come before the changes were made. Together the monthly checks were not enough to pay a long-term care facility, but because savings and checking accounts were now closed, Mother qualified for Medicaid assistance. The checks would go in entirety to the home, and Medicaid would make up the balance. In return, Mother would receive a few dollars for personal needs each month.

But everything came to a standstill. I couldn't get the hospital doctor to *release* her until I could get a local doctor to *take* her. Not knowing which community's nursing home had a vacancy, I couldn't even consult a local doctor to *ask*. I couldn't give the bank, railroad, or social security an address until she *had* one. And social services couldn't begin to do its part until I did mine.

After driving more than 150 miles, I'd had enough for one day and arrived back at the hospital in time to feed Mother her supper. There I was greeted by a visitor who expressed surprise that I'd left Mother alone! I was entering a strange new world. And more than ever before, I was aware of how much I needed God's help.

3

You're Gonna Do *What?*

WELL, AT LEAST THE DOCTOR WILL HELP ME get Mother released to a nursing home when I find one," I comforted myself, relating the previous day's experiences to the social services lady.

Abruptly she stopped taking notes and looked at me skeptically. To my dismay, she related that regardless of his promises, this doctor had never helped an elderly person into a home. No wonder I "just missed him" each hospital visit, even though I left at midnight or after and returned before dawn.

I made an appointment at his office, where I waited a long time to see him. He refused to sign anything to discharge Mother from the hospital to the nursing home, paradoxically offering, "But I'll help you any way I can."

"It's some kind of hang-up with him," said his nurse after he exited. "I don't know if he made a vow to himself or someone else or what, and I sure don't ask. But he won't sign."

That was to be my introduction to what I call the "nursing home syndrome," the stigma of being the next of kin.

Mother couldn't even feed herself, so she couldn't stay alone. I couldn't handle her, so I couldn't take her. He couldn't release her except to a nursing home, but he wouldn't do it. What a feeling of helplessness!

Suddenly I began meeting people who weren't in my shoes but seemed to know what I should do. Because of my easygoing nature, they proceeded to tell me. A favorite old saying of Mother's was proving correct time after time:

"If advice cost anything, there wouldn't be so much of it given away."

I'd had enough hints. I should have guessed what I was facing.

*   *   *

"Whatever are you thinking of? As sick as she is and going to send her by ambulance for some test!" one visitor had snapped in disbelief earlier in the illness.

"You're going to kill her! If she was *my* mother, I wouldn't think of such a thing!" (Could this be the same friend who previously chided me for not being pushy enough to get something done?)

I had really debated over the test, but having seen Mother lose ground so quickly, I decided to do anything that might help. The test was available only in New Orleans.

Surprised at the vehemence in the lady's voice, I answered, "Well, I've decided that I'd rather look back and say, 'I did too much,' than 'If only I'd done more.'"

"Hmmmph!" she grunted, shaking her head as she left.

The next morning the ambulance driver was so kind to Mother and me. I sat in front with him, and we talked. His own mother had been through a hard time, and he seemed very understanding. It felt good to have someone who knew what Mother was going through and what I was feeling as well.

The trip was without incident, and Mother didn't even know she had gone. The test showed good brain activity.

But criticism was just beginning.

*   *   *

Because I wanted a nursing home near Mama's town, I began my quest for a permanent physician in that area. I found one who was said to be faithful in treating nursing home residents, and I sat down with the office manager.

She began to ask questions and fill out forms. All went well until near the end, when she came to the information for the next of kin.

"What is your complete address and phone number?" she asked in a businesslike but semifriendly way.

When I told her I lived in Memphis, I couldn't believe the change that came over her. She threw her pen down on the desk, folded her arms across her chest, and jerked back away from me.

"Do you mean to tell me you're going to stick her in the nursing home here in Louisiana and run off and leave her while you live in Memphis?" she hissed.

"But this is her home," I said, choking up, feeling as if I'd been slapped.

"But you're her daughter!" she almost yelled with contempt.

"Yes, I'm her daughter, her only child," I said brokenly, fighting tears, "and I have to work. Here is where her friends are, her church, her world—"

"Her only daughter, her only child! I don't understand how you can run off to Memphis and leave her alone. You ought to take her to Memphis, where your precious job is, and you could go to see her after work."

"You don't understand," I pleaded. (Family caregivers often try to explain everything. I know better now.) "She knows no one in Memphis. There'd be no one to visit her."

"She knows *you!*" she sneered.

I tried to explain that, as a speaker, during speaking season I would be on a driving tour up to six weeks at a time, or flying in and out between driving. But she heard nothing except what she wanted to hear.

There was already that feeling of unreality that comes with the long time of tending a loved one, the indescribable fatigue that causes the mind and body both to ache, a sort of fog and fear that envelops the very being.

This can't be happening, I thought, as the room grew dim and I struggled to keep from fainting.

She completed the form, shaking her head. (I became very good at causing head shakes.)

I left crying as I drove the long road back to the hospital for my vigil. Around midnight I drove back to Mama's home for a restless few hours to try to prepare for the next day before returning to the hospital. Between breakfast and lunch, I drove back to Mama's home parish and found that her previous physician was willing to take her on again and make the necessary nursing home visits. He said he was in and out of the homes several times a week. That proved to be an exaggeration, and we later changed doctors to meet the state's requirement of a once-a-month visit. But on this day it sounded good.

Nervously, I approached the office I'd visited the day before and retrieved the papers and records I'd left with them. Fortunately, someone other than the rude office manager helped me.

When I returned to the hospital, there sat Vivian and Gloria, two of Mama's precious friends who, despite their own health problems, came to visit and, finding Mother alone, stayed until I could get back. There is no greater earthly gift than friendship that asks no questions, offers no criticisms, renders no judgment, but is just simply there. Thank God for the Vivians and the Glorias, always kind and helpful.

Other friends like Nicky and Bill, men who commuted to jobs near the city where the hospital was located, gave up their lunch hours to check on Mother. When finding her alone with an untouched tray of food about to be removed, they fed her. It is interesting that these two men never came to visit on the same day and never met each other.

Talk about knowing that God sent help! And those weren't the only times I felt His loving concern through friends.

4

The Search Begins

L ET'S KEEP OUR EYES AND EARS OPEN for anything and everything," I told Bill's wife, Myrna, as we approached the first nursing home on our inspection tour.

Myrna had cooked extra during these weeks to leave a meal for me to find en route home from the hospital at night. Now she volunteered to go with me throughout several communities to find a nursing home. We didn't make appointments but tried to blend in naturally to see the real operation.

The first one was brand-new and professionally decorated—more like a four-star hotel with spotless, large, well-lighted rooms. But there didn't appear to be a range of social classes or interaction among the exceptionally well dressed residents. There was a sense of aloofness present, although we observed the staff to be kind and friendly.

At the time I honestly did not expect Mama to live very long, but I wanted her to be comfortable. I couldn't imagine her with her print dresses and country background in conversation with many of these people. And if her health improved, she would need to talk or "bust," as she often said. There were a number of vacancies, but the cost was beyond our limitations, even with help.

We left the beautiful, quiet facility and went to another—a very attractive building with wide halls and plenty of windows. There seemed to be more activity there, with some residents walking about and talking. A calendar listed numerous events. Workers seemed warm and well liked. It was impressive but had no vacancies.

Another home was under beautiful oak trees with giant limbs that seemed to spread forever and decorated themselves with flowing Spanish moss. What a setting! But the same beautiful oaks that adorned the outside brought darkness inside. Even with the lighting, a kind of gloom sat upon the whole interior. When we walked in, we were greeted with silence. Most of the residents just sat, not noticing us. So did most of the staff. We roamed uninterrupted and, when ready to ask questions, stood waiting while idle employees discussed a soap opera. Myrna and I looked at each other, simultaneously saying, "Unh-unh!" There were no vacancies anyhow.

After hours of visits and phone calls in several cities and parishes, we made our last stop. Being located near Mama's town, this was the one I had called first. Because of its long waiting list, I had been given no hope and had left it until last to visit.

This nursing home was a rather plain, long brick building. But people were crossing the parking lot that adjoined with the hospital next door—interesting to watch. This was especially nice, because many seemed to know each other as locals and waved or stopped to chat. The rooms on the back side faced trees and pasture with a number of grazing cows.

Flower beds in full bloom lined the building front. A recessed patio also had several flower beds in it. Residents seated in wheelchairs and lawn furniture welcomed us with warm smiles and hellos. Upon entering, we were greeted by a receptionist who offered assistance. This place was really racking up the points!

A game was being played in another area, and laughter followed us down the hall. A bulletin board exhibited photographs of smiling residents participating in various activities, both in-house and on field trips. One banner proclaimed "Mr. Evans, Bowler of the Week" with his score alongside. A large calendar had nearly every day filled with a choice of activities and occasions. There was something for everybody. But what about Mother?

She prided herself on never having had a deck of cards in her hands, so I knew bridge was out. She never sat still, so table games wouldn't excite her. Bingo she'd associate with gambling. But church services were listed, and even a couple of nights of gospel singing. Uh-oh! There was a live band and dancing—better not let her see that one!

There were a number of craft times, and the activity room door was ajar, showing several residents creating all sorts of goodies from whatnots to a big dollhouse. The man building the dollhouse was a stroke victim and was working with only one hand.

Everything was clean. Aides and nurses smiled and spoke with the familiar, warm "How ya doin'?" Only those residents who were bedfast were in nightwear. All able to be up were dressed and well groomed. Many were mobile, and I mean *mobile!*

"Can you believe this?" Myrna's voice revealed her excitement. "Some *young* people don't have this much stuff going on!"

So we agreed: "This is the place." But, of course, there were no vacancies. And this time it mattered.

I put Mother's name on the waiting list, again hearing it could be from weeks to months or longer. Most likely any opening that occurred would mean someone else had lost a loved one.

These weren't just rooms to me. Mother and I had visited friends here, so I was thinking "people." I really prayed for a room to be vacant, but I didn't want it to come about through another family's grief. I didn't quite know how to pray, now that our own need was so great, and time was of the essence.

But how often I'd been reminded of Rom. 8:26: "Likewise the Spirit also helpeth our infirmities: for we know not what we should pray for as we ought: but the Spirit itself maketh intercession for us with groanings which cannot be uttered."

Back at the hospital a kind aide suggested that I put Mother's name on every waiting list in every home and take the first opening anywhere. "But keep her name on the list of the one you really like. When a vacancy comes, you can always move her. That's what we did with my grandmother. You have to do something, and in the meantime this will give you more time to check each place again and talk with relatives of residents. It never hurts to talk to the residents themselves either. See how they really feel."

Social services asked if I'd explained the urgency of the case: "If you tell them the doctor won't release her from the hospital except to a nursing home, they'll probably move her name up. If there's nobody else with that priority, and a vacancy occurs, they'll fit her right in."

Well, I thought I'd stressed that. But for much of my life I'd tried to exercise the strictest discipline over showing my feelings. Perhaps my quiet nature and calm appearance had worked against me.

Sure enough, all the places we'd called and visited and I'd revisited alone had entered Mother's name at the bottom. So I started with the home I preferred and retraced my steps. This time my self-discipline failed.

"Oh, I didn't realize you need a room right away," social workers apologized.

Even the home that seemed the most promising and had the longest waiting list moved Mother's name to the top, expecting an opening within a few days. The very next day a resident left the nursing home to live with relatives, and I was notified of the vacancy. At last we were on our way. And no one had died to make it happen.

*   *   *

The move was not complicated except emotionally. I'd

discussed it again and again with Mother, making sure I had her approval. We knew the doctor had said it would be permanent, but we also knew he didn't know Mama! So she added the clause, "If this is what it takes, I'll do it. And it'll be permanent until I can take care of myself."

This helped relieve some of the terrible pressure I was feeling. It's strange how these things work with us humans. We do all we can do. We endanger our own health. We know it's the only choice. And still the guilt sets in.

Friends who knew the situation encouraged us in our right decision and promised to keep visiting and calling. Those who hadn't kept up with the extent of the illness were harshly critical. Could they be correct? Was sending her to a nursing home really sentencing her to death?

The ambulance driver who'd been so friendly and talkative on our other trip now just glared at me and never spoke another word, not even acknowledging my appreciation for his gentleness with my mother.

After seeing her safely moved, I walked slowly down the hall of the nursing home and out the door. I'd never felt so alone and so guilty. There seemed to be cement blocks tied to my feet, they were so heavy—and so was my heart. My throat ached as I fought tears and held back screams of emotional pain.

Seated on the patio in a glider with her mother was a lady from our town. We'd met only once, but when she saw the stricken look on my face, she hurried to my side.

Resting her hand gently on my arm, she said, "Kathryn, it's never easy. We do what we *have* to do."

And giving a little squeeze, she added, "I'll be praying for you and your mother."

A kind word or gesture from friend or stranger is precious beyond measure.

Written many years ago but still so timely today is Prov. 12:25, "Heaviness in the heart of man maketh it stoop: but a good word maketh it glad."

5

The Stay

THE MORNING AFTER MAMA'S MOVE from the hospital, a Sunday, I slept until after sunrise, and the nursing home still hadn't called—a good sign. I dressed and drove the short two and one-half miles to visit Mother in her new location. Residents and staff greeted me pleasantly, and I was feeling better all the time—until I rounded a corner near Mother's room.

Aides were scurrying along the corridor and through her doorway. So many people were bending over her bed that my view was blocked.

"Oh, no," I whispered. "This is it."

Fearing the worst, I froze and waited.

Suddenly, the crowd burst from the room. It looked like a soft drink spewing from a shaken bottle.

Aides and nurses were gathered around something they were hovering over and pushing. I expected to see Mother's lifeless form under a sheet, but instead I found them laughing and joking with a scrawny little lady upright in a wheelchair. She was so weak that her head kept bobbing. It took me a few seconds to recognize the shrunken face with its big grin—it was Mama!

She had rested well but awakened with no memory of the ambulance ride from the hospital. All my talk preparing her for the nursing home had been for nothing. She thought she was still in the hospital but in a different room that faced a pasture of cows. On this morning, without heavy sedation, Mother was already regaining interest in life around her.

A body brace over a new housedress kept her from doubling over, and a security tie kept her from falling onto the floor. What hair she had left was in a little bun, and someone had even remembered her glasses. She may not have known where she was, but she knew she'd done something big—even if she wasn't sure what. The reason for the crowd was that it took quite a few to lift and dress her.

Of all places for them to take her—the TV area! Mama felt the same about television as she did cards and bingo. She might not have known she was in the nursing home, but she did know she was in the room with a television set. And it didn't make any difference that a church service was in progress on the big screen.

With skilled care the aides tried to encourage the residents and had everyone who was able to be up dressed in Sunday best and rolled out for "church" and fellowship. I explained to Mother that it was known she loved church—but not how she felt about television.

"Even if you don't want to look at it, you can listen to the music and the sermon until you're able to attend a service in person," I coaxed.

"I probably don't even believe in their doctrine," she mumbled, weak as she was.

She couldn't stay up long and soon began to beg for her bed. Each day she was to sit up a little longer and thereby regain her strength.

That afternoon a stream of hometown visitors began to arrive, none staying long enough to tire her.

At first she was mostly bedfast, in diapers, and unable to hold anything of weight in her hands. She was restricted to a salt-free diet, but she didn't tell that to her guests when they asked what she'd like them to bring her. She'd answer innocently, "Some dill pickles would be nice."

Feeling empathetic, friends brought pickles of every

size and description—from home-canned slices in half-pints to store-bought whole ones in gallons. Mother had each person put his or her jar in a different place among her belongings, so no one dreamed what a supply she actually stored! The first time I walked in and saw Mother hiding behind a pillow with her mouth puckered around a forbidden pickle, I didn't know whether to laugh or sigh. And when I reorganized the chest of drawers and wardrobe, I found quite an assortment of full and empty jars. I could see that my independent little mother was going to bear watching!

*   *   *

I wrote postcards to relatives and friends throughout our ordeal, keeping them updated on Mother's condition and location. Encouraging personal mail began to arrive as people were faithful to write. But once again I met up against the "nursing home syndrome" with two of Mother's close childhood friends.

They had been included with each update I sent out. After all, the three had exchanged letters across the years and states. When I sent them her address, I explained that she was too weak to write back but had been asking about them and that it would be a big boost for her to hear from them.

Perhaps their own fears of helplessness and nursing home confinement kept them from writing the friend they loved so dearly. But neither friend responded until Mother herself was finally able to write.

*   *   *

Medical bills were pouring in, and I was out of time. As a fledgling speaker, I *had* to keep engagements that were confirmed long before I resigned as professor.

Speaking is unlike the type of job that allows an employee to use vacation days in an emergency, maybe even getting someone to substitute. When a speaker is slated, often several years in advance, the hosts invest a lot of time, expense, and effort in promoting the special occasion. To cancel would result in major scheduling problems for the hosting organization and a blight on the speaker's dependability. It would also mean a loss of income. Mother and I were not accustomed to such bills, and now to feel the sudden deluge of them—well, I *had* to work.

Because this was the beginning of my new career, I drove to most of my speaking engagements, often hundreds of miles each way. My next date was a three-week tour, meaning I'd drive to a certain state, be housed in a central location, and go out from there to speak in different areas for miles around.

I dreaded leaving her for so long, but Mother was improving rapidly. Her appetite was growing, and she was being exercised gently but routinely. She had graduated to the bedpan during the day. With her care facility being in her home area, she was receiving visitors every day. She understood I would be in and out between work at the church in Memphis and speaking engagements.

Although she still couldn't sit up alone, I praised her for each little accomplishment she made. "I don't want to get your hopes up too fast or too high, Mama, but you keep up with every exercise and help yourself in every way you can. Remember—if and when you can walk, we'll try you at home. If and when you can cook for yourself— you can go home." I made sure she had everything she needed, gave my itinerary to the staff, and with my heart torn, I left.

Mother couldn't hold a phone receiver yet, so I made regular calls to her nurses. I wrote to her even more often than the once a week to which she'd been accustomed.

Now on this longer driving tour of about 3,000 miles,

Mother was still on my mind as I gave my best to my work. In addition to speaking, hours were filled with traveling, praying, studying, writing, recording, and appearing on television and radio. This didn't include the hours I stood after appearances greeting and listening to the people who'd just listened to me, enjoying their comments and sharing their burdens.

So I really didn't feel I deserved what happened next.

In a large city on my circuit, one of Mother's two long-time friends was in my audience. During the break I located her and began working my way through the crowded auditorium to reach her. Finally at her side, I tapped her on the arm to get her attention. It felt good to be near someone from Mother's growing-up years.

This friend had not seen me since my childhood, and thus far she'd seen me only in costume during the first session that had just ended. I had redressed as myself and soon would be introduced to speak in the second session. Calling her by name, my hands outstretched in greeting, I introduced myself.

"I'm Cecil Price's daughter, Kathryn," I said, smiling.

To my surprise, her own smile disappeared, and she snatched her hands back. Arms rigid at her sides and jaw set firmly, she stared up at me through narrowed eyelids before pouncing with a cutting, "When are you going to quit all this running around and go home and take care of your mother as you ought to?"

My mouth dropped open as hers snapped shut. And now I had to return to the platform and try to be inspirational! Here I was working my heart out, and she thought I was vacationing while my mother lay ill.

Afterward when I was alone, I thought it through. I recalled her past letters to Mother about her son who would disappear for months or more at a time. She'd be nearly sick with worry that something had happened to him. Finally, destitute in some distant state, he'd call collect, saying he wanted to come home to see her. From her small pension she would send a money order or bus ticket, which he often used to prolong his spree. She thought herself an authority on what Cecil's child should be doing, but when it came to her own child and his complete disregard for her, she was blind.

I wrote Mother about seeing her friend but never mentioned how hatefully she had acted. I've experienced her kind of rudeness periodically, but it always catches me off guard. In comparing notes with other nursing home families, I find this is common and most often comes from those whose own children have little or no contact with them—that is, until a need arises.

At the time I thought I was the only one ever treated in such a manner. Thank God, these hurts were lessened by many overwhelming expressions of love and support from wonderful people around the country through cards, letters, phone calls, and face-to-face comfort. They came from long-term friends as well as new acquaintances, although I purposefully never mentioned my own problems from the platform.

When the tour was over, I drove directly to Louisiana and was delighted to see Mother's progress. I still could not handle her, but when leaving for Memphis a few days later, I promised to come back as soon as I could.

I threw myself into my work at the church, trying to make up for the time I had been away. But true to my word, I returned to Louisiana on my first opportunity. Mother had begun writing and was excited about our attempting an overnight at her home. However, her walking was limited to only a few steps while being held up by two strong aides.

Upon our arrival to the duplex that was home, two neighbor men lifted Mother from the car onto a kitchen chair and carried her to the bedroom. I had completely re-arranged the furniture in a close-knit circle to accommodate her visit.

After seating her in the big platform rocker, I brought in our Chihuahua, Joy. The two hadn't seen each other for several months, and little Joy, one front paw poised in mid-step, stared at this stranger. When she heard Mother's voice, however, she gave a mournful cry, and her little feet slid out from under her in her haste to reach Mother's chair.

In a few minutes Mother was weary and needed to rest. I squeezed between her and the chair and slid down into the seat with her. My arms clasped around her waist, I lifted our combined weights with my legs as I stood, inching a slow turn that allowed me to sit on the bed with her between my knees. Balancing her, I crawled backward onto the bed as I lowered her into place. Then I climbed over her to get back to the floor. She broke her long-standing rule of "no pets on the furniture" and asked for Joy to join her. There they lay contentedly side by side in a peaceful nap.

By eleven o'clock that night—and countless liftings onto the potty chair, the rocker, and the bed—Mother admitted she wasn't ready to come home. But I assured her we'd keep trying.

I spent most of the next day after her departure washing and cleaning. As hard as we tried, we still were not able to avoid "accidents," which had touched everything within reach. I was glad she realized on her own that she was not able to return home yet. She was disappointed but more determined than ever to work toward regaining her strength and moving back.

6

Home Awhile

K ATHRYN JOYCE, WITH MY WALKER AND AN AIDE I can walk 15 feet now!" Mother kept me apprised of every single inch she gained.

Her recovery began slowly, because she exercised only in her room, refusing to go along the training rail in the hall because she would have to hear the TV. As I had feared, she never left her room—even to attend the provided church services, since they were "probably a watered-down gospel" from which she wouldn't get any help. She planned to wait until she returned home so she could go to her own church, where they weren't "afraid to preach it straight."

She was so used to staying busy that the idleness was making her grouchy. But again, a dear friend came to the rescue.

Myrna visited Mother one afternoon on her way home from teaching first grade.

"Mrs. Martin, I'm just wondering if you're planning to do any more crocheting," she half asked as she dug into her purse for something.

Mother's curiosity was aroused. Myrna pulled out a little crocheted boot just right for a Christmas tree ornament.

"A friend gave this to me with jelly beans in it, and I'm thinking what a nice gift this would make for my little students. But you're the only one I know who crochets. Could you make something like this?" Myrna asked, not dreaming she was about to change Mother's life—and mine.

"Well, if that's not the cutest little thing!" Mother caught the vision. "I don't know if I can do handwork anymore or not, Myrna, but if you'll get my crochet needles and some yarn, I'll give it a go."

Within a few days all 28 little boots were completed. The work brought in admirers along with orders for more little boots. Meeting such nice residents brought her out, and her walking increased as she exercised with renewed vigor.

Shortly thereafter, social services told me that Mother had about reached her potential. My thoughts were confirmed when I was informed, "If she has to wait very long to go home, she'll start losing ground."

I knew my schedule wouldn't permit me to care for her during the critical weeks of transition. Again I felt torn, knowing Mama needed me but unable to disregard the commitments I'd already made. But this time my concern proved unmerited, because Mother had long before secretly arranged for my aunt Bernice to come from Oklahoma to be with her. What a reflection of Mother's determination!

It was such an answer to prayer when Mother, in the nursing home only seven months, made her departure. I thought she hardly had a chance of recovery, yet here she was crocheting and ready to enjoy her sister's company as they relived old times.

*   *   *

Aunt Bernice cooked and waited on Mother generously for quite a while. But when Mother seemed too content with this arrangement, Aunt Bernice announced, "Cecil, I have cooked my last meal. From now on you are the cook." And she sat down.

So Mother began cooking again and doing more for herself. Soon I was able to take my aunt home.

Mother gradually grew stronger and was able to function on her own. I kept her pantry stocked, and friends picked up extra items for her on their own grocery days. They also took her for her doctor's appointments.

Church members who passed nearby provided transportation so Mother could attend services. Her excitement and enthusiasm to return to her familiar routine of church attendance, even in inclement weather, produced frequent colds and pneumonia. She was in her glory, but I could tell she wasn't always at her best.

My travel had now increased and was from coast to coast and into Canada, mostly by air. However, I was still fulfilling earlier slatings that were within driving distance.

Sometimes I would arrive home in Memphis too tired to unpack. On a number of these occasions, early the next morning I would receive word Mother had just been taken to the hospital. The proverbial burst of adrenaline would get me unpacked, repacked, and on the highway for the seven-hour drive. In a day or so Mother would become chipper and would be discharged. When I began to notice she was never hospitalized during one of my speaking tours and I never had to cancel an engagement because of her hospitalizations, I realized Mother was also a victim of our arrangement.

She would hear criticism: "It seems like a long time since Kathryn was here. I don't know how she can be taking these trips all over the place and not come live with you. If it was my daughter, I'd *make* her come and take care of me."

"But she's off working," Mother would say, coming to my defense. "She has to make a living, and she's helping me. Besides, she's answering God's call on her life. I wouldn't have her change that for anything."

"Well," they'd retort, "all the same, it doesn't look right."

Mother would get so upset over all this that she actually would become sick. Being admitted to the hospital would assure her I was soon to arrive. Eating right and seeing visitors, she would improve quickly. But the crowning achievement was that I was there. It made no difference whether I had just been there for a visit or already planned to be there within a few days. The end result showed Mother's critical friends that her daughter could be depended upon.

Except for those hospital episodes, we were able to operate rather smoothly for several years. But eventually Mother's situation began to change.

Sometimes she would act confused, not completing a sentence but just stopping short a word or so and leave it dangling with an "unhunh" on the end. My concern was aroused, but I would relax when on my next visit she was bright and talkative.

These incidents began to occur more frequently. She had done well for so long. Now my concern grew into speculation about what was happening: weather extremes, improper medication, and poor nutrition. My suspicions were on target for all three counts.

"Mother, have you been running your air conditioner?"

"I run it," she answered smugly.

"Mother, are you running your air conditioner now, right this minute?"

"I run it," she repeated.

"But how *often* do you run it?"

"Oh, come off it, Kathryn Joyce—you make me sick keeping on asking the same old thing. Yes, I run it."

My frustrations built as I sought an answer. "Mother, I need to know," I continued asking as she continued to evade me. "Is your air conditioner on right this minute?"

"Kathryn Joyce," she answered disgustedly, "I put it on when I need it."

"But do you need it right now?" I was in tears and

raised my voice to get an answer. "Mother, this is the worst heat wave this country has had in years. Young people in their 30s are dying. The news is warning everybody, especially older people, to stay inside and run air conditioners if possible."

"I don't need an air conditioner! My window fan is all I need." (I shouldn't have mentioned the news, because that meant it came from TV—enough to make her ignore the advice.)

I visited Mother often—especially considering the nature of my full-time job involving travel and the many miles separating our homes. I had been there in the summer when the south Louisiana climate reached temperatures in the high 90s or more than 100 degrees (with a humidity to match). I'd scrubbed enough mold and mildew off walls and furniture to realize exactly why her lungs were in such a condition and she contracted pneumonia easily. Even doctors had cautioned her to use air-conditioning—if not for cooling, at least to take the dampness out of the air. One doctor even forbade the use of her big window fan, which pulled in even more spores and dust harmful to her lungs.

"Mother, it's a must for your health."

"All right," she laughed. "If it'll make you feel better, I'll turn it on."

The way she spoke told me she'd probably turn the air conditioner on and right off again so she'd be truthful. Her neighbors confirmed that for me.

With the house so hot, visitors were fewer and less frequent. Some told me they couldn't stand it anymore; they had suggested turning on the air conditioner, only to be told, "Kathryn Joyce is always after me to run that thing, and I don't need it. I don't get hot like some people. I never sweat."

When I'd arrive for a visit, I'd be hit in the face with

the musty, moldy dampness of the house. Even the piano shed some of its beautiful finish. Slides and books were ruined with mildew.

During the winter I experienced the same ordeal with the heating. When I arrived earlier than expected, I found the house terribly cold. Sweat dribbled down the walls and stood in puddles on the floors. The sheets were as damp as if removed from the clothesline before drying. I tried to convince Mother to leave the heat on low all the time, but she would turn it from suffocatingly high to completely off. During the cold nights she slept with no heat at all, getting up often for the rest room or just to crochet if she couldn't sleep.

Then I discovered she changed doctors each time her friends did, thinking she could feel better. She was annoyed that each new doctor wanted to run tests, then give prescriptions.

"But what else can a doctor do?" I asked. "They can't treat you until you've been thoroughly examined. Then all they can do is prescribe medicine. It's up to you to do what they recommend and take care of yourself."

Her cabinets were filled with medicines from different doctors. Sometimes she'd get gung ho and take a mixture of them. Other times she'd say, "I can't see that medicine is doing me a bit of good," and quit taking all of them.

The assortment of healthful groceries I provided her was most often untouched. She preferred to buy chicken backs, boil them, and eat them day after day. For vegetables she'd open a can of spinach and eat the entire contents straight from the can. Then diarrhea would set in and become uncontrollable. That would precipitate using a strong medication that made her drowsy. With the loss of important body fluids similar to that which had crippled her, now through sweating and diarrhea, she was sluggish and couldn't finish her sentences.

She still used a walker to get about and couldn't always make it to the portable toilet in time. She had kept a very clean house and thought she was continuing to do so. But her mopping was only smearing the floors, and the odors were becoming more potent.

Because she was weaker and had not been able to stand alone since the back surgery, Mother often propped on the stove while waiting for her coffee to warm. So I should not have been surprised when I noticed the burn holes in her sleeves.

"Mother, how did those holes get there? From the stove?" I asked.

"Oh, it's nothing," she chuckled proudly. "Now and then I lean on the stove a little too long, and they catch fire. But I just 'slap, slap' [she demonstrated with both hands frightfully near the burners] and put out the fires."

I felt that familiar sick feeling in my middle, and my fears were about to be realized.

7

Moving Again

"Hello," I said as I answered the phone late one evening.

From the other end of the line came shuffling sounds as the caller fumbled with the receiver.

"Hello, hello!" I called cheerfully.

"Kathryn Joyce," Mother croaked, "where've you been? I've been trying to call you all day. Unhunh, unhunh. I'm awfully sick, Honey. Unhunh, unhunh. Why wouldn't you answer? Unhunh, unhunh."

My throat tightened. Working in the office since early morning, I'd received a number of long-distance calls, so I knew Mother had been unable to dial through. She sounded awful.

I finally managed to have her hang up so I could call a neighbor to check on her. Sure enough, she was feverish and disoriented, her bed soiled from sweating, nausea, and diarrhea.

With less company and excitement, she had created unnecessary chores around the house and yard. This included painting the back steps in extreme heat and perspiring so much that she dehydrated and felt chilly. Thinking the weather had cooled, she shut windows and doors, lying in the closed-up house while outside it was actually 102 degrees with a humidity of 100 percent.

In the hospital it took several days of replenishing her body fluids and regulating her medicine for her to be a semblance of her old self. And at each visit her doctor was talking "nursing home."

"Your mother is one of these people who just can't stop," he said. "She is determined to live alone but can't realize that at 84, with her health history, there are things she should never attempt. Most people her age would enjoy just 'being,' but she's got such spirit she's got to be 'doing' as well. I can't impress her enough about this, but if she wants to see 85, she's going to have to do it in a nursing home."

Already at the door, he spun on his heel and came back to me. "It wouldn't do a bit of good if you moved someone in with her—or even if you yourself did. She's going to do what she wants if it kills her, and it almost has!" He ended with a grin of frustration, and I knew just how he felt.

From her hospital bed Mother brought up the subject of the nursing home and surprised me by saying she thought she'd go back in. I think it was from a combination of things. She was bored and knew there would always be something going on there. She loved people and would have more visitors. And deep down inside I think she realized she just couldn't take care of herself properly anymore. This would be a new adventure, and she wouldn't have to stay if she didn't want to.

I began to make arrangements—only this time I knew more about what to do, starting with social services. They called the nursing home, whose worker was then expecting me when I arrived. Knowing that Mother would be sent directly from the hospital, the worker gave us one of the first vacancies.

It just so happened that the parish social services representative was making her regular visit that day, and I was able to start on the paperwork with her as well. These forms were about Mother's assets to determine her eligibility for Medicaid assistance again. She had been on her own with her railroad widow's pension and social security checks while home.

It was also necessary to visit the bank and check the amounts in her checking and savings accounts. Then I went to the insurance company and funeral home to learn the value of burial policies Mother held. Her prepaid plan at the current rate for an average funeral was considered an asset. Therefore, in order to qualify for Medicaid, she could not hold a bank account with more than $200. By the time I took care of prescription items, medical balances, and the first month's stay at the nursing home, that wasn't a problem. Mother's funds were gone again.

What helped tremendously, however, was something Mother did long before her first nursing home stay. She decided to transfer the deed of the house to me so that when she died, there wouldn't be any legal hassles. I really discouraged her from doing so. Besides, as the only child, there wouldn't be any problems if she died first.

But for once, Mother's self-sufficiency paid off. She went through her files and totaled just a fraction of what I had spent on medical bills for her and Daddy through the years. She took her proof to a lawyer, who then drew up papers showing that Mother sold the house to me for that amount. I learned of the sale when Mother sent me the clipping from the court news column of the newspaper.

"It's only right," she protested when I rebelled. "All your life you've done for me, and when we lost your daddy, you took care of that too. You never have asked me for one thing. And while other young people have been out looking after their own needs, accumulating something, you've been spending your money on me. As far as I'm concerned, you bought the house a long time ago. The only difference is that most people sign the papers first, then buy the house. The way I see it is you paid in advance and will sign the papers last." And she refused to back down.

If she hadn't been so adamant and the house had still been in her name, I would have been forced to sell it and use all the funds before benefiting from any Medicaid assistance.

But by then Mother might have been ready to leave the nursing home without a place to go. Also, on all the trips I made to be with her or care for her needs, I would have found myself without a home as well. Thankfully, she took care of all this in advance.

To complete the parish forms, I verified the exact amounts of her checks and that she had no other income or dividends. Also I listed her Medicare, Medicare supplement, and ambulance insurance premium amounts.

I was given a sheaf of papers from the nursing home informing me of expectations, both theirs and ours. Theirs covered furnishings such as room, care, and personal services. They agreed to arrange hospital transportation when the physician ordered and to notify me when it occurred. My obligations were to supply personal clothing, expense balances, and extra spending money.

One form gave us the freedom to choose whether we'd like to donate any unused catheter or internal feeding supplies if these treatments were started and discontinued. Another form was our authorization for drugs to be ordered from the pharmacy of our choice, accepting financial responsibility for anything not covered by Medicaid. Two sheets of paper listed staple drugs the nursing home would provide, such as aspirin or its substitute, rubbing alcohol, and various ointments and laxatives. Others authorized the assignment of benefits to those who furnished medical services.

If all relatives had time to peruse this information well in advance and compare various facilities, some of the stress of a committal would be alleviated. But more often than not the sickness comes as Mother's former one did— unexpectedly. The pressure is so great that decisions must be made all too hurriedly.

This time I felt like a veteran. I knew now that we were fortunate to have such an excellent offering of nursing homes right in our locale. Being in a smaller town, not much escapes attention. Friends and relatives with watchful eyes come and go at varying times. Owners, directors, and staff members are well-respected people from the area. Newspapers and radio stations keep alert of any nursing home happenings.

From past experience we knew which nursing home could meet our needs. I signed all the forms I was to sign, and this time Mother didn't need an ambulance. I borrowed a wheelchair and rolled her across the adjoining parking lots to the nursing home office. There a nursing home staff member addressed her questions and comments to Mother personally and not to me, well pleased with her mental alertness and ability to articulate.

She asked about hobbies and interests as well as physical needs. Then she read each statement from a page of residents' rights as she looked directly into Mother's eyes, making certain everything was understood before she checked it off and continued. This covered such things as the right to receive mail and visitors, to practice religious and civil liberties, to be free to complain or suggest without fear, to manage personal affairs if able, to be treated with dignity . . .

Then Mother was ready to be admitted. She looked to me to sign her in as the lady held a pen outstretched.

"No, Mama, I don't have to sign," I said, smiling. "This time you're able to make your own decision and sign for yourself."

That was to be one of the wisest things I ever did.

Getting Adjusted

K ATHRYN JOYCE DIDN'T PUT ME IN the nursing home," Mother boasted to visitors. "I put myself in here."

She was proud of that, for it meant she was still in control. She could sign out anytime she wanted, whether for a few hours or for good.

Mother was well matched with her roommate. Not only were Mama and Miss Lillie near the same age, but also they had similar interests. Both could quote long portions of Bible passages, songs, and poems. Some of Miss Lillie's poems she had written herself.

Both were farmers. Mother lived in town but had always had something growing. Until her recent stroke Miss Lillie had her own strawberry farm that she'd run without modern utilities. The two ladies were to plant and harvest many a crop from their beds at night.

Mother regained her strength more rapidly in her efforts to use her walker and help Miss Lillie, who was very limited in movement. The biggest essential in Mama's life was to feel needed. Now she would be fulfilled again.

* * *

Hoping to get Mother out of her room for a while, I told her I'd go to the afternoon service with her Sunday.

"Honey, I'll just wait until I feel better and go to my own church," was her reply.

"Well, Mama," I persisted, "I've got a surprise for you. I wasn't going to tell you until we got there. You know

Spencer's church is the one coming today, but they're without a pastor. So Spencer is going to fill in."

That changed everything.

Mother had been friends with Spencer and Lillian since moving to Louisiana. They'd met as neighbors. During World War II, Spencer had gone off to war, and Mother took his young wife and daughters under her wing. Times were hard while he was missing in action and a prisoner of war, so Mother took food, clothing, and lots of encouragement with her on visits.

Just in case letters could reach him, she wrote Spencer regularly, giving neighborhood news and assurance of his family's well-being. His one reply that made it through to her became one of Mother's treasures. It expressed his appreciation for her friendship and care of his family during his absence.

Recently Spencer shed more light on the bond between them. Apparently Mama suddenly sold the farm where she and Daddy once lived—*without* talking it over with Daddy. The sale was to Spencer and Lillian, because she wanted to help them get a home of their own after the war.

Spencer also gave important information about how Mother's health eventually became so poor: "Your mother had us soldiers on her heart so strongly that she couldn't do enough during the war. She made trip after trip to New Orleans and volunteered in every way she could, from rolling bandages to making up packages to send overseas. She even made trips especially to give blood. She got sick one day while donating, and when the nurses checked their records, come to find out she'd been giving way too often. They forbade her to give any more. But it seemed as if her health never was too good after that."

Also Spencer and Lillian were responsible for having their doctor find Mother's problem of potassium depletion during her earlier long hospital stay.

Just mentioning their names was enough to get Mama raring to go to the service. That Sunday afternoon I borrowed a vacant wheelchair and wheeled her to the dining room, where church services were held. She glowed as other residents from the town recognized and welcomed her.

I played the piano and sang "How Great Thou Art" in a ladies' trio. Spencer brought the message. Mother was proud of us, and that added to her enjoyment of the service. It also marked the beginning of her regular attendance at nursing home church functions.

Occasionally a wheelchair wasn't available, so she would miss the service if she didn't feel up to the walk. But that didn't happen too many times before Mother showed great elation during one of our regular phone visits.

"Guess what!" she said excitedly. "Spencer and Lillian just bought me a wheelchair! They said they wanted me to have wheels and not have to take turns with the community chairs. So I can go anywhere I want to now!"

When I offered to pay or even help on the cost, I was met with sweet resistance. "After all your mother has done for us down through the years, it's a privilege to do something for her," they insisted.

This wonderful gift with its sense of restored freedom opened new doors to further adventures for Mother and more ease to my mind. She happily used her laundry pen to scrawl in big, uneven letters "CECIL MARTIN" along the sides and back of the brand-new chair's upholstery.

Because her lap was usually full of something or other on her way to do who knows what, she never had free hands to wheel herself the way most people do. Instead, she kept the footrests up and pulled herself along with her feet. The "swoosh" sounds of her slipper soles preceded her.

*   *   *

Most Sundays during the first year or so of her nursing home experience, Mama would roll herself to the front door and park her wheelchair with the row of others whose owners were gone for the day or weekend. She'd use the walker to cross the last few yards to the outdoor patio, always arriving early to keep her ride from waiting. When I was in my early teens, Mama bought a car and supplied many rides for others, often going out of her way and being made to wait. Now she didn't want to be guilty of inconveniencing anyone, so she again fought colds and pneumonia that came from exposure.

After the wait, early arrival, Sunday School, morning worship, and altar service, she would frequently return to the nursing home too tired to eat. She would try to rest that afternoon and go back to church that night. She even tried to attend Wednesday night services and revivals. The routine many people take for granted was exhausting to her, and she'd have to stay in bed most of the next day or two to recover. She became slower and slower in getting around and felt she was a burden to those who stopped for her.

"Mother, the Lord knows your limitations," I reminded her. "He doesn't expect us to do things that make us sick. Just as you never took up any habits that were bad for you when you were younger, neither should you continue to push yourself now when you know something affects your health. You've reached an age where you can't do everything you used to, and the Lord knows all that."

"Well, Kathryn Joyce," she answered worriedly, "I feel as if I need to be there. It's encouraging to other folks when they see how old I am and how my health is, and yet I still go. But sometimes I just feel as if I'm not going to make it. My back hurts so bad sitting up so long. Plus I don't have as much control over my kidneys as I used to. I go to the bathroom before my ride comes and stop at the ladies' room at church. Then I go again between Sunday School and morning worship. Sometimes I'm miserable if the preaching is long and especially if there's an altar service. I've never soiled the bench, but I sometimes have an accident before I can get back. I always wear those pad things so I won't mess up anybody's car."

"Well, Mama, I think your day is just too long for you. How about asking if someone could pick you up just in time for either Sunday School or church but not both? Just tell them the facts," I advised. "They'll be understanding."

"No, Honey, I can't do that," she countered. "Sometimes I think I'm putting them out just to stop for me. I'd never ask them to make a special trip back."

In the meantime, she was using her wheelchair to visit more church functions in the nursing home.

"Monday afternoons the ladies' group from Spencer and Lillian's church brings a short devotional," she reported enthusiastically. "Afterward they serve us cake and cookies and are sweet to sit and visit. Then on Friday mornings a lady from another denomination comes and teaches Sunday School for those who won't be able to go out. But I enjoy it too. Then some Saturday afternoons another group comes and has a service with lots of singing."

The nursing home church services and social functions were kept to about 30 minutes, and Mother could manage those. But some Sundays she just couldn't endure getting in and out of cars and three or four hours of being up. Reluctantly, she went out less and less and relied more often on the in-house services.

"I can't agree to everything that's preached," she said, "but I just take out what I need and don't say anything about the rest."

It was at one of those services that another exciting door opened. At starting time the song leader said, "Our piano player couldn't make it today, so we'll have to sing without the music. That is, unless we have a piano player here. Does anyone play?"

"Mrs. Martin plays," someone volunteered.

"Well, come on up if you don't mind and help us out, please, ma'am. We sure need you."

The leader and other residents made over the playing of this 84-year-old, and she was frequently called on to fill in after that.

Her loves, church and music, were helping her make other adjustments to nursing home living, and she was beginning to enjoy life—although still on a limited scale.

Her room became more homey as I followed her instructions and took more and more of her possessions to her. I had a phone put in her room so she had the freedom to visit more comfortably with friends who could not come in person. When the phone would ring, she'd look at her clock and say, "That'll be [the person's name]. She calls every day this time to check on me."

I sent her new number to friends and relatives who lived a distance away, and they started their surprise calls. Her letters were filled with, "You'll never in this world guess who called me last night!"

(Sometimes after numerous attempts to reach Mother without an answer, friends would call the nurses' station outside her room to see if Mother was sick. Her response: "I told you I don't *live* in my room—I just *sleep* in it!")

Her days became fuller. On bath days (Tuesdays, Thursdays, and Saturdays) she'd grow restless at having to wait and would make the remark, "I can't be waiting until seven or eight o'clock in the morning—I've got other fish to fry!" So the "bath aide" began to call Mama "Fish Fry" and would pick her up for bath and whirlpool from 5:30 to 6 A.M.

All these events contributed to a change in Mother's condition. Her general health improved rapidly. The disoriented thinking and confusion disappeared. Friends and staff members began to rely on her for facts from past events or future plans because "Mrs. Martin never forgets." The interaction with others, in addition to the controlled temperature, balanced diet, and monitored medication, was helpful mentally and physically. The security of having medical help as close as a pull cord in the bathroom and call button at her bedside led to peace of mind.

I encouraged her to participate more in social activities, so Mother began attending the monthly birthday party and the occasional Saturday night country gospel group. In addition to her established friends, workers and residents came to her room, bringing their families to meet the "crochet lady" and enjoy a chat. The director of activities popped in one day and, admiring the crochet work, asked permission to send two pieces to the parish fair.

Mother had never been to a fair, having heard it preached against as worldly, and grew quiet. But the director explained that a large variety of crafts would be on display, so she gave in. They selected a Christmas candle, complete from holder to flame, crocheted from red, green, and white yarn. Also chosen was a doll whose beautiful crocheted pink dress disguised its purpose as a spare toilet-tissue cover.

Before long Mother said, "My work is back from the fair, and I don't intend ever again to let anybody borrow anything. Somebody's stuck safety pins and ribbons on both of them!"

"Ribbons? Mama! Where are they? They must have entered in the fair and won!" I was so excited.

"Yep," Mother said nonchalantly, "she said I won. I stuck them in the drawer."

"Mama, they need to be out for people to see!" I rooted for the two pieces and found a blue ribbon on one and a red ribbon on the other. At 85 she'd won first and premium places and was fussing because somebody stuck pins in her work to hold the ribbons on! She received so many congratulatory remarks over those ribbons that she never put them away again.

I enjoyed sharing with Mama gifts I received so she could set them out as conversation pieces. (Not that she needed them!) If it was a craft-related item, she often created her own rendition of the object.

One such item was a little animal head made from three squares of plastic canvas. Two tiny eyes were glued to its green yarn exterior. Hanging from it was a little tag reading, "Squeeze my cheeks and I'll give you a kiss." Sure enough—squeeze the two sides, and a red mouth opened, offering a chocolate kiss.

I bought the canvas, and Mother went to work. For a long while afterward, every phone call and letter reported how many she had made and how many she had sold or promised. But she never once abbreviated it, always using the whole name: "Those little 'squeeze my cheeks and I'll give you a kiss' things."

Mama had an unbelievable amount of company. Her pastor visited weekly. Friends from church and miles around came by often. Relatives drove great distances to see her. And now that word of Mother's crocheting and crafts spread, she was really having company. She was filling orders for ornaments, baby bonnets and booties, doilies, Easter baskets, and even a couple of tablecloths. Tenderhearted, she never priced items very high and often *gave* them away. No one ever left empty-handed. That was a joy of Mother's life—filling people's hands one way or another.

Residents began taking clothing to her for altering or mending. She could rake through her button jar to match (well, *almost* match) buttons for their shirts. She even kept an awl with which to punch holes in men's belts as they lost or gained weight. When they wanted to pay her, she'd say, "I couldn't take your money. And besides, I might have to call on you for something sometime."

Then those she helped shared gifts of fruit, candy, or something that was given to them. Indeed, a most-appreciated gift to a nursing home resident is something that can be shared.

Now Mama had become the "sewing lady" as well as the "crochet lady" and ventured into the activities room to see what else was going on:

"I helped dye Easter eggs, and they let us eat the broken ones. I'm so tired of eating eggs."

"I volunteered to make a pillow for the bazaar, and I've finished it. The proceeds will go into the activity fund. My friend promised an afghan, but she's having trouble; so to encourage her, I told her I'd do 24 of the 50 blocks, and she can do 26. With her doing over half, she'll feel like it's still her work."

When someone took cloth remnants to her, Mother got back into quilting on a small portable frame that Lillian ordered for her. She made herself some patchwork modesty aprons to cover her legs, as her dresses tended to ride up. She also made gifts of baby quilts. Lillian gave her a frame on which to weave place mats, and she launched into those by the dozens. Mama's thoughtfulness was returned as gifts of homemade jellies, crocheted baskets, and other goodies were brought in or mailed to her.

"Bless their hearts—the Easleys are so sweet to me. They're regular as clockwork to visit, and they always bring something. He takes me to vote, you know, and never tries to influence my voting."

"That plaque with the pretty verse plays music. Barbara Ann [her godchild] brought me that."

When I exclaimed over an expensive floral arrangement, she said, "Oh, that's from my friend in California. I met her when she came to visit her mother and told her not to worry after she left as I'd keep an eye on her mother."

For a change of pace, Mother visited residents confined to their rooms and played a few pieces on her keyboard, Autoharp, harmonica, or kazoo. She entered a spelling bee, and she and my third grade teacher, Mrs. Coburn, 94, were the only two left standing—or in this case, left sitting.

She joined the Saturday morning sing-alongs, because the activities director "plays records of the old songs and really knows how to work with those old folks." She became even perkier when she started exercise classes. Memorizing the routines, she continued to exercise on days the classes didn't meet. The exercises were adapted to the local interest in the Sportman's Paradise State: "Raise that arm and cast that line; now pull that big fish in."

Mother was living it up. After one of her fun-time sessions I learned why.

"Today we were each supposed to tell what we'd done for fun as young people. I sat there like a knot on a log with nothing to tell when it came my turn. My folks were so strict, we children didn't know anything except working in the fields and the house. We weren't allowed to have friends over to play, and on Sundays we just sat—first at church, then at home. When we started courting, Mama would call us in from the porch: 'Bedtime, girls—say goodnight and come on inside.' It wouldn't even be six o'clock in the evening yet, and the sun still high in the sky.

"So today I was the only one who didn't participate," she said, reflective and quiet for a moment. Then she looked up with a grin and finished: "I guess that's why I'm having so much fun in here—I'm making up for nearly 86 years!"

Yes, she was beginning to enjoy life more. But neither

she nor I could envision the even more dramatic change that was about to take place—one that would give her a whole new outlook and me my first gray hair.

9

Courtship and the Coming Out

KATHRYN JOYCE," MOTHER WHISPERED from her wheel chair. "Sit on my bed while I close the door. I want to tell you something."

Glancing furtively out into the hall, she eased the door shut and rolled back to me, peeking to see if Miss Lillie was still napping.

"I was introduced to the nicest man today to help make him feel at home." Exuding excitement and wonderment, she clicked her thumbnails together nervously as she added, "Later in the church service here he came in and *sat* with me!"

She looked ill at ease and pleased at the same time. It was the same look she would have a few weeks later when she told me, "I loved your daddy—but this man is a *fun* man. I hope you don't mind, but . . . I'm in love.

"Of course, he's a younger man. I'm 86 and he's only 83."

"Age doesn't mean a thing, Mother," I said, telling her what I believe and what she needed to hear. "A person never gets too old to love or be loved. If more people realized that, there wouldn't be so many lonely folks around."

"Well, most tell me they think it's sweet we've got each other. But old Miss Know-it-all said she didn't see a thing sweet about it. She thought it was disgusting at our age. But one of my friends spoke up, 'The only reason you think it's disgusting is because you wanted him first, and he never looked in your direction.'

"I told her I never set out to get him, but now I've got him, she'd better stay away from him!" And with one abrupt nod of the head, Mother clinched it as fact.

As the courtship progressed, the two lovebirds grew closer and closer, and conversations were filled with their dream of marriage.

"I just know we could make it, Honey," Mother tried to convince me with every reason she could muster.

"Our health is better. We could live at the house. He's strong enough to walk the block to the grocery store. I'd have to give up a portion of my railroad widow's pension, but we'd still have enough between our checks. Cousin Joe [then 96] said he'd even give me away. You just think it over, and I'll do whatever you say." The words tumbled out nonstop.

"Mama," I interrupted, "I want you to be happy. But let me look into it and see what I can come up with. We still don't know much about him, and we don't want to rush into something so serious."

I knew she wasn't going to drop the subject, so off I went to investigate.

Mr. B.'s praises were sung by everyone of whom I inquired. "Such a gentleman!" "He's so polite—and handsome too." "You notice how healthy he seems? He takes long walks around the home and doesn't even get breathless."

Then I talked to someone who knew the details of the medical situation and confided in me:

"Kathryn, let them have their good time, but discourage marriage. Mr. B. is much sicker than he looks, but he doesn't know it. In six months or so he is going to be a lot worse off than your mama, and you're really going to have your hands full."

Then the blow came, and I felt sick: "He's got Alzheimer's disease." She paused a moment. "Miss Cecil is a sharp lady, and if you tell her soon, she won't get her hopes up. She's strong. She can take it."

I dreaded my task, but, finding Mother alone, I broke the news to her.

"Well, Honey, I can take care of him. I took care of your daddy when he got down. And besides, isn't there some medicine I could give him? And he'd probably get better when we got out on our own. He says he feels better when we're together, and I know I do." She clicked her thumbnails pathetically.

"Mama, Daddy was down only a few months, and it nearly finished us both off. This could go on and on." I reminded her of the resident who had taught school for years, yet one day she couldn't remember how to get home.

"Soon she couldn't figure out how to get back inside her house from her own mailbox. And when she started roaming, she'd be found a long way from home in the middle of the street or the railroad tracks. Her husband was a strong man, and even he couldn't handle her anymore. She hasn't recognized him for several years, although he comes faithfully every day.

"Mr. B. is a muscular fellow. How would you ever be able to stop him if he walked off? You can't even walk yourself without holding on to the walker or furniture. Whatever we do, let's not let on to Mr. B. about his condition, or he might give up hope. I think the best thing to do is live every day to the fullest and enjoy each other while you can." I said it as tenderly as I could.

Mother was disappointed—greatly disappointed—but she hadn't given up. With characteristic determination, she seemed driven to meet and conquer this new challenge that threatened her future. She plunged headlong into living.

"Kathryn Joyce, I never dreamed a person could have so much fun," she wrote, sometimes at midnight or after.

"Our days are so full I don't have time to write anymore unless I wake up during the night. We go to everything together, except the playing bowling. He's been good to go to all the church services with me but is so used to being active, I know he misses his bowling. So I told him I wouldn't feel bad at him if he started playing. He wants to teach me, and I'm in a quandary, as I've always been told it's wrong."

"Mama," I wrote back, "I think bowling must be like a lot of things that started out as good, clean games but wound up in questionable places. It wasn't the game that went wrong but the activities and places that surrounded it. Now that's changed, and I know church people who bowl with their families and friends. And I just can't think there'd be any games allowed in a nursing home that would be wrong."

Soon I read, "I made him feel so good today. I watched him playing bowling. And you know, Kathryn Joyce, I couldn't see anything wrong about it. They just move the chairs and tables out of the way in the dining room and put down these white plastic milk-bottle-looking things, and you take this big ball and throw it and see how many of those milk bottle things you can knock down."

Sure enough, the next Thursday Mother ventured into "playing bowling," and it wasn't long until her excitement turned to a mixture of pride and dismay. "I beat *him* today. I wanted to make him proud of me, but I didn't intend to make better than he did. But he just beamed and said how proud he was of me."

Shortly after that when I asked about bowling, she said, "I got the highest score of everybody this week—37." (When you consider that 40 was the most anyone could get, that's terrific!) "So now my name is up on the big banner as people come in: 'Cecil Martin, Bowler of the Week.'"

"Mama, that's wonderful!" I cheered.

"Yes, one time when I threw that ball at those milk-bottle-looking things, I knocked them all down at once," she added innocently.

"Mama, that's great!" I nearly yelled into the phone. "I think that's what bowlers are really trying to do."

"Well, I wondered why everybody clapped for me," she mused. "You know, I could have done even better, but the next time I went to throw the ball, I caught my sleeve on the arm of my wheelchair."

Mother and Mr. B. were involved in so many activities that she wrote, "You know, I can't see where he has any symptoms of that disease. His mind is just as good, and he's still going strong. Don't worry, as I won't do anything against your wishes, but I think they've made a mistake in their diagnosis.

"I just wish he and I could have a little more privacy," she added. "I'd like sometimes just to sit with him alone without people gawking at us. What do you think about us going over to the house and spending the day?"

I wrote her back to say that as long as Mr. B. wasn't wandering off, it'd be fine with me. But remember—Mother had signed herself into the nursing home. By the time I sent my approval by return mail, they had already been to the house! An aide who had become like a family member used her day off to transport Mother and Mr. B., checking the house and helping them inside.

Mother wrote me with the details: "We had the most wonderful time ever. He pulled the rocking chair by the back door, and with me beside him, we watched the martin birds soaring around the birdhouse you got me. It was so peaceful. I fixed our coffee. Then later we ate the picnic lunch the kitchen worker had sent with us. I hope we can do it again."

They were to enjoy a number of these special times at the house. As promised, they remained inside and took no chances on the steps or the thick Saint Augustine grass into which I feared Mother's walker might sink and trip her.

So life was full and wonderful, and people watched from far and near to see what would happen next.

10

Not All Peaches and Cream

WHILE ALL THIS WONDERFUL NEW WORLD was opening to Mother, everyday life in the nursing home was still going on with its normal ups and downs. As with any large group of people living under one roof, there has to be a certain amount of regimentation, or there will be chaos. Having been on her own so many years, Mother didn't always see the necessity of such order.

When she was required to begin eating in the dining area, she resisted, almost with fear. She could talk to anybody anywhere at any time, but, to my surprise, to eat in front of people was really upsetting her.

Like many others, she had been ill upon arrival to the nursing home and was served in her room, accepting it as routine. With so many residents bedfast and needing special help, it benefited everyone (especially residents, kitchen staff, and aides) to have those who were ambulatory to go to a central location. For several days she fought indigestion until she realized that her table companions were more interested in the dinners than the diners.

*   *   *

Because a nursing home is a community within a community, the same kinds of people live, work, and visit as in the outside world: the good, bad, and indifferent. One satisfying distinction is the continual effort to protect residents against the bad and indifferent.

Miss Lillie's chocolate candies were disappearing quickly, so Mother cautioned her against eating too many.

"But I've had just a couple, Mrs. Martin," she pondered aloud. "I think somebody's taking them."

Her niece added, "If it weren't that Aunt Lillie might get them, I'd slip some chocolate-flavored laxative in with her chocolates. That would teach them!"

They laughed over the thought, but that night the two roommates lay in their beds, narrowing the time of day the candy jar emptied fastest. Soon Miss Lillie drifted off to sleep, but Mother had plans and got up.

"I dumped the candies out and counted them twice, noting the time. Then I replaced the candy, tightened the lid, and went back to bed—pretending to be asleep.

"It wasn't long before the new aide we suspected slipped in to check the room and perform her duties. As soon as she closed the door behind her, I got my glasses and walker and counted the chocolates again.

"Sure enough, they were three short. I knew we had the culprit. The next morning I went to the proper person with my testimony and was told that the nursing home had suspected this woman of other thefts but didn't have enough proof. 'Now you have your proof,' I said."

The worker, confronted with facts, admitted her guilt and was gone a lot quicker than she had come. Reputable nursing homes will not tolerate theft in any manner. Signs to that effect are usually posted prominently enough to discourage the very idea.

But Mother felt rather exposed and requested locks to be installed on at least two drawers. As the maintenance man finished the job, he handed Mother a key and said, "I guess you'll want to leave the other key with the nurses, won't you?"

"Well, I guess I won't," she said as she grabbed the other key. "What's the use of having a lock if half the country has a key to it?"

And those two drawers were soon loaded with valuables—that is, things valuable to Mother and her friends. Items of monetary value were left with nurses to lock away, but items of heart value were entrusted to Mother. There were such things as a man's $1.99 quartz watch that didn't run anymore but was a gift from his grandson. One lady's scissors, often misplaced, were there to be found easily. Most touching to me was the little worn coin purse with a house key its feeble owner hoped to use again.

To protect these goodies and more, Mother kept the drawers locked and wore the key pinned to her cotton slip.

*   *   *

Physical maladies often interfere with everyday life—especially in a nursing home.

"Sometimes I can hardly move," Mother wrote. "Old Arthur Ritis just won't leave me alone. I put my crochet needles down and think I'll have to give it up, but a few days later I'm back at it until my hands hurt again. When I wake up, I can't seem to wiggle until late into the morning. But when I ask the Lord to help me and I stir about, I usually find somebody that's worse off, and I get to feeling better."

"Sometimes my left leg doesn't want to let me go, and I can't use my walker at all. Even to get in the bathroom, I have to roll in my wheelchair."

"I've felt so bad lately I've just stayed in bed. People miss me and come by to check on me. They know I must be sick, or I'd be out among them."

"Oh, I'm so glad there's a better place to go someday, where my body won't be in pain."

*   *   *

Of course, troubles were not limited to the physical. Gone are my illusions that older people have it made spiritually.

"The devil tries to make me believe I never did have any religion. I tell him to go away and leave me alone, for I didn't start out all those years ago to give up this close to the end."

Other things added to this distress. When Mother's health limited her attendance to her own church, a woman who had recently moved to the area made the statement, "You old people ought to be in church. This is not right!"

Mother was so upset that she was sick in bed for two days.

"Mama, she had no business saying that—she wasn't even here to see how far you've come," I sympathized. "She's young and in good health. Just wait until she gets a few years on her and an illness or two. We'll see how much going *she* does!"

Mother's thumbnail clicking was in high gear. She said, "I told her I went until I could go no more, and now I go in here; but she said that it's not the same, that this is not really church, and I'm not hearing the truth—that I could go if I put forth the effort."

Three days after this setback, Mother was all bubbly again. "I prayed and thought a lot about what she said. And I came to the conclusion that if I was able to be in outside church all the time, I wouldn't need to be in here in the first place.

"And in the second place, when I get to heaven, there won't be any denominational church signs out front. So her rules won't count anyhow!" And with one of her curt nods, that ended that.

*   *   *

I passed along every message anyone ever sent to my mother except "Tell her I'm coming to see her."

People mean well when they say it, but with today's hectic schedules, "next week" has a way of never quite arriving. So I always told her whom I'd seen and who asked about her—but left off mention of the promised visit.

Mama was blessed that very few days passed without numerous visitors, both drop-ins and regulars. Yet I've seen residents, including Mother, sit in their rooms for several days—missing activities—to watch for a guest whose good intentions weren't good enough. Wiser to say nothing and make the visit a surprise instead of a disappointment.

"You wouldn't believe all the pastors and church people who come both to hold services and to visit around," Mother wrote. "They don't just burst into our rooms, but they knock and ask if we'd like to have them come in and have prayer. Some say that if I need them, day or night, to call. I think that's so nice. And there are clubs galore that come and have special activities or refreshments or gifts." (She'd never thought much of clubs.)

That was better than "We sat and waited the other day for a group, and they never did show up. They forgot about us."

*   *   *

Food. I've not seen an institutional setting yet that didn't have complaints, no matter how good the food.

Letters and phone conversations were filled with "We had the best meal just now: baked chicken, mashed potatoes, green beans, and pudding." Or, "For breakfast I had a biscuit, jelly, eggs, grits, and bacon."

So it surprised me when the complaints started. Realizing many residents were used to the heavily seasoned French dishes typical to the area (complete with the roux—special dark gravy that's a basic in so many meals), I knew the sudden change to bland diets was unusual. But I was there to witness the change in food quality and knew something was wrong. (It is worth the small cost to order a meal in advance and eat with a loved one occasionally.)

"Some of the residents asked me to go and speak up for them about the food at the residents' council meeting, and I intend to do just that!" Mother vowed.

"Just say it nicely, Mama," I advised. "There's a way to get these things done. First, you want to remark about all the good food of the past. Then, gently call attention to the change, with examples. Tell them you've been asked to represent many of the others, and that all of you appreciate whatever's being done to correct the problem."

Armed with a "fresh" piece of corn bread that felt hard as stone, Mother bade me farewell and was off to the regular meeting of residents and administration. When her turn came, she completely disregarded my advice, dumped the corn bread on the table with a "clunk," and launched into her spiel.

A resident who had been the worst to complain was asked if she felt the same way.

"Oh, no," she backed down. "I think the meals are just wonderful! Just wonderful!"

"Just wonderful, my foot! See if I talk up for you anymore," Mother fumed. "It makes me look as if I'm the only one fussing."

But it became obvious to residents and families that there was a problem, and it wasn't very long until changes were made to ensure good meals once again.

*   *   *

At times the very thought of change has to be overcome. As the roommates improved, Mother was moved to a more active area, and Miss Lillie realized her dream of returning to live near her beloved farm.

Because Mother's move was the nursing home's decision and not our request, the staff moved her belongings, and the establishment paid the telephone relocation charge. The new setup was composed of two rooms with two ladies each and a bathroom between for all four.

"Hmph!" Mother griped with a quick grin. "Even I would have better sense than to make four old ladies all in wheelchairs and taking fluid pills share one bathroom!"

As soon as another room with private bath had a vacancy, Mother was moved in with Miss Dot, a quiet lady who loved to read and was partially paralyzed from a stroke. Mother couldn't understand why anyone would rather stay in a room and read when there was so much else going on, but the two ladies looked after each other, exchanging favorite foods from their trays or sharing what visitors brought. (Many families take extra treats to include the roommate.)

Miss Dot and I hit it off right away. In fact, she paid me one of the highest compliments possible in the Deep South—she asked me to call her "just plain Dot." We are taught from childhood to use "Mr." or "Mrs." with someone's last name and no more familiarity than someone's first name preceded by "Mr." or "Miss." And always, regardless of social standing, the polite "ma'am" and "sir" is expected to be used when addressing anyone older than ourselves.

While this may not be applicable in all situations, nursing home residents usually appreciate being able to maintain a sense of dignity by signs of respect like these.

*   *   *

Sad things happen—especially in an environment such as a nursing home.

"Anna got confused for the first time last night. She thought she was a little orphan girl again and came into my room, begging to sleep in my bed with me. She said she wouldn't take up much room, that she didn't have a home."

Through tears Mother explained that her bed was too little for both of them, but that Anna had her own bed now, and everything would be all right. Mother called an aide, who escorted Anna to a special tucking in.

When deaths occurred both in the home and out, Mother would grieve but accept. She no longer went to wakes or funerals, but instead wrote her own sympathy letters. When I was in town, I'd attend, and beside my name on the registration I included "also representing Mrs. Cecil Martin" so she still felt included.

Often health improves and residents leave for their own homes or that of relatives.

"My friend that I mended for and enjoyed talking to left to live with his stepchildren this week. He's the one that brought me little jars of decaffeinated coffee because I wouldn't charge for sewing. I'm happy for him, but I feel blue for me."

*   *   *

Humor is an important aspect of nursing home life.

Wheeling down the hallway, Mother called out to a fellow about to leave his room, "No, no—go back, go back!"

Looking startled, the usually well-dressed man finally realized he was fully clothed—except for pants.

"I just kept right on a-rolling," Mother said seriously, "as I didn't want to embarrass him. But I could tell he didn't know which would be better—to back up or turn around!"

From the hallway with the doors closed, many rooms look alike. So each room has the names of its occupants attached to its door and a one-of-a-kind poster nearby to help the resident identify his or her own place.

Half asleep while coming from the TV area one evening, a man mistakenly stepped into the room of one of Mama's friends.

"What are you doing in my room?" he asked brusquely.

"What am *I* doing in *your* room?" she fired back. "What are *you* doing in *my* room? Get out—yours is across the hall! Get out! Get out!"

The next day when her friend was laughing about it, Mother said, "You beat anything I ever saw! Here you just told me recently you wish you had a boyfriend too, and when one comes right to you, you throw him out!"

Once a new aide made diaper-check rounds about two or three in the morning.

"I'd been asleep a long time, dead to the world," Mother said as she relived the experience. "All of a sudden I felt a hand on my bottom, and I jumped and let out a yelp. I scared the girl so badly she screamed and jumped back and hit the wall and almost fell over my crochet stand. She started apologizing, and I got so tickled that I could hardly get the words out that I take care of my own needs and don't wear diapers anymore. When she saw how well I took it, she commenced to laughing too, and we laughed so hard I hurt. I've laughed this livelong day." And she was still so tickled she could hardly relate her story.

*   *   *

Eventually Mother spent so much time up during the day to be with Mr. B. that her legs were terribly swollen. The calves of both legs became infected from cuts made by constant contact with the wheelchair footrests.

"I was sitting in the TV area with him, working on my puzzle book, when old Miss Nuisance came rolling by. She just goes around and around the place in big circles. I told her, 'Here—move on away. I just got out of the hospital from my legs being hurt, and I don't want to go through that again.'

"She didn't pay me a bit of mind, and every time she came back around, she bumped my chair. I put a stop to it, though. I rolled up my big, thick puzzle book you bought me with the circle-the-words and popped her on the arm."

"Mama!" I gasped. "Did you hurt her?"

"No, I didn't hit her hard enough to hurt her—just hard enough to let her know I meant business."

11

The Cage Door Opens More

MOTHER, WHO HAD WRITTEN THE BOOK on strictness, was tearing out its pages one by one.

"Kathryn Joyce, I sure hated to hear about Jack dying," I heard long-distance.

I'm pretty good with names, but I couldn't think of anyone she and I knew in common with the name of Jack.

"Jack who, Mama?" Surely I hadn't forgotten someone.

"You know, that announcer on the program where they spin the wheel." She still wasn't *watching* television, but she couldn't help but *hear* Pat Sajak tell about it. And to think Daddy sat alone when he watched his few programs.

I was now overhearing terms of endearment I'd seldom heard her use at home when I was growing up. She was "Baby," and he was "Honey," and I was "Nearly Invisible."

"Fan me with a brick," she flushed. "Last night he told me good-night and walked away. Then he turned around and came back to me and kissed me! I hope nobody saw."

Soon afterward, another visitor and I fell in step going down the corridor.

"What's this I hear about your mother having a gentleman friend?" the lady inquired.

Before I could say anything, we rounded the corner just in time to see Mr. B. lean over *my mother's* chair, kiss her soundly, say good-bye, and head our way. We tripped over each other in our haste to back away without being seen.

"Well, I guess that answers *that* question," we giggled.

Life was so good that Mr. B. gained back the pounds

lost during his illness, and Mother was struggling to keep her weight down. He was still wanting to get married, and Mother was still trying to exercise caution, although she would have said "I do" in a minute if I had approved it.

Letters were filled with pride as he had been selected "Most Handsome Man" and was now gone to the beauty pageant among the area nursing homes. Local stores had supplied a gray tuxedo for him and a gown for their "Most Beautiful Woman." Mother supplied his haircut and mustache trim, admonishing me to bring my electric clippers next time I came so I could start cutting his hair. Never mind that a cosmetologist was there regularly at reduced rates. Mother wanted to save him money.

Mr. B. returned with a trophy and later went on to the district level, where he won another. He was more happy that Mother was proud of him than at winning. So for display, the trophies were taken to Mother's now crowded room.

He had arrived at the nursing home with very few possessions because of a burglary while he was hospitalized for an operation in a distant city. Those trophies were the only things he had to offer her. So they were especially dear.

One Tuesday evening I answered the phone to hear Mother's excited voice. It alarmed me, because *I* usually did the calling.

"No, nothing's wrong," she assured me. "Did I wait until the cheap time to call you? Well, Kathryn Joyce, this has been the happiest day of my whole life. It was too good to keep until you call on Saturday.

"This morning the aides came and got us and said we had to hurry to get ready. They even put my best dress on and combed my hair again. They were just grinning from ear to ear and said he and I had been elected king and queen of the nursing home Mardi Gras!"

I congratulated, feeling both thrilled and shocked, for in south Louisiana Mardi Gras is such a big event that schools dismiss and many businesses close. But Mother had always viewed the festivities as—well, you can guess. And now here she was the *queen* of them!

"What must I do?" she had asked.

"Just wave and smile, Mrs. Martin—wave and smile," was the answer.

She and Mr. B. were cloaked in royal purple robes, crowned, and handed scepters as they headed the Mardi Gras Parade of the Krewe of Elders.

She was pushed in her wheelchair, and he walked beside, both waving and smiling and waving and smiling some more to those who lined the route and those who watched from their rooms.

The parade ended back in the dining area, where the band played as Mother and Mr. B. displayed big smiles that would appear in area newspapers the next day.

Saturday morning when I called, she was still overflowing. "Oh, Kathryn Joyce, I never knew I could be so happy!"

Knowing she'd had a tremendous week emotionally as well as physically, I wondered if she'd be able to go out to her own church the next morning.

"No, I don't think I'll go," she said thoughtfully.

"Are you feeling bad?" I pursued.

"No, I admit I *am* tired." She paused. And with a wisdom befitting her years, she tried to stretch that magical week out as long as she could by saying, "But I don't think I'll go. I figure he'll preach against the Mardi Gras."

12

Mama Taking Care of Business

JUST IN CASE WE CAN GET MARRIED, there's something that really needs to be taken care of beforehand" was the next thing I heard on the agenda.

Mother flitted from one idea to the next, much like a bird hopping from one branch to another.

"He doesn't have any money put back for burial, and I don't want that to be an expense for you if he becomes your stepfather."

Mr. B.'s policies had been stolen during the burglary, and he couldn't remember the insurance companies. So Mother decided to appeal to his Masonic lodge. That's right: he'd been a faithful Mason, and r-i-p—there went another page from the "secret organization" part of Mother's strictness book.

Cousin Joe, the 96-year-old, got the address of the temple for Mother to write of Mr. B.'s plight. When the Masons didn't answer in two weeks, she wrote again. I don't know what she wrote, but I *do* know that the Masons didn't just call—they came! She was jubilant at the results of the visit.

"Kathryn Joyce, we won't have to worry anymore. They will conduct the services, and they bought a small policy here that the funeral home agreed to accept as full pay. Praise God for answering my prayers! Now, the next thing I want you to do . . ."

(Did you ever feel like running away?)

Our family burial plot was purchased long ago. Therefore, the only place for Mr. B. was at Mother's feet. They didn't care, just so they could be together. (I wondered what Daddy would think, lying over there to one side!)

"But Mama," I said, laying down the law, "this is it. You know, men sometimes die first. What if this fellow dies and you get *another* boyfriend? We could have little men buried all over that cemetery!"

She assured me this would be the only man for her.

In the meantime, after sketching our cemetery plot with grave sites drawn to scale and labeled, I left copies complete with funeral plans in their files at the nursing home, funeral home, and city hall. I promised I'd take care of everything—with the understanding that if Mr. B.'s family came and had other plans, I would step aside.

Then the two began saving for perpetual care of their graves—and would I please see to it that he had flowers through the years. I wondered if I wouldn't beat them both to the cemetery!

"Now if I just could know his heart is right with the Lord, I could relax," Mother said, worrying. "He's such a good man, but it takes more than being good to make it to heaven."

"Well, Mama, that's one thing I can't take care of for you," I said seriously but with a smile.

His salvation meant so much to her that she began requesting prayer for him through anyone she knew who prayed. Without pushing, Mother never let an opportunity slip by to discuss the subject with him, while she kept praying for him with a deep burden. Except for this one area of concern, all was well.

*   *   *

As her social life grew, Mama's physical problems dwindled. She found it annoying to wait in her room for her doctor to make his monthly visits.

The medical expenses shrank. Her only regular medication was a diuretic tablet. When occasionally she'd need something else, the thoughtful physicians prescribed generic drugs or something Medicaid would help cover. Mother insisted upon using her crochet money to help with unpaid balances, and I assumed the remainder.

There were times when, weary and discouraged, I wondered why Mother had so many medical treatment and pharmacy balances when other residents with larger incomes had theirs paid by Medicaid or written off by the suppliers. And Mother even carried a supplemental policy most residents didn't.

As her needs lessened, I learned there had been a computer error. Mother had actually qualified for Medicaid even during her first big hospital stay. It was still in the computer but never carried through to completion. Our ignorance of the situation was little consolation for my assumption of those years of medical expenses—or for Mama's use of her little crochet funds.

*   *   *

Meanwhile, the nursing home was saddened by the loss of the stroke victim who built dollhouses and delivered the mail around from room to room.

"I don't know how they'll ever replace him," Mother said. "He was such a kind, friendly man. Everybody loved him."

Her next letter said, "I've been delivering the mail for a week now. The secretary sorts it and marks room numbers. I carry a little cardboard box on my lap and wheel from room to room."

Updates were frequent: "I know 125 people's names and room numbers now . . . I figured out if I deliver to the dining rooms to those up and about, they come early to wait so I'm not in the way. It saves me going in and out of rooms except for those who are room bound. Friday is my hardest day, as that's when the *TV Guide* comes." (Mama delivering *TV Guides!*)

We nearly fought once when I tried to assist. I wanted to organize the mail by room numbers, and she wanted to "look through" as she shuffled along, going according to names—often resulting in retracing her shuffles if someone changed rooms.

Meanwhile, because Mr. B. liked *As the World "Goes Around"* and the noon news, Mother used that time to deliver the mail so it wouldn't hurt the romance.

"When I roll through the TV area on my route, I pat him on the arm, and he just smiles and says, 'Hurry back to me, Baby.'" She beamed.

And that's how the crochet lady, the sewing lady, the piano lady, and the courting lady became "the mail lady."

13

Busyness Taking Care of Mama

"THERE JUST AREN'T ENOUGH HOURS IN THE DAY!" Mother exclaimed.

"Oh, Kathryn Joyce, Honey," she apologized often as we met in passing, "I just hate to run off and leave you, but if you can wait about 15 minutes, he and I will be right back." Their calendar was so full that some days I'd have to make three trips to the nursing home to catch her for a visit.

"Whether he has that disease or not, we may neither one have that long. But I've asked the Lord to give us at least two good years." And trusting the Lord, Mother set out to pack that two years full.

I now lived in Louisiana more than Memphis, turning my attention and energy to full-time speaking. The pastor in Memphis with whom I'd worked retired and joined me in my work. A widow with grown children, Jacklyn Welch Shockley became not only my cowriter but also cospeaker. We were often slated as a team, and in traveling across the country, it helped to have two headquarters.

Because there is so much behind-the-scenes work in speaking, many hours are spent in office work. Mother's duplex lent itself well to serving as both home and office. Often I took my breaks by running up to the nursing home—lying on Mother's bed waiting for her and enjoying a visit with Dot.

Their room was peaceful. Outside the picture window

across a narrow, grassy lawn was a small stand of trees and undergrowth. Squirrels and birds ate from the two feeders I hung in view. Beyond the trees, black-and-white Holstein cows grazed in a rich, green field. Amid them, long-legged white cattle egrets fed on insects and sometimes caught a ride on the backs of their namesakes.

Inside, the window ledge was filled with potted plants, and the tops of chests were lined with gifts, trophies, and craftwork. Across the bed was a beautiful, bright, multicolored afghan. On the walls were more gifts—nature scenes that artist friends painted for Mother.

Also hanging were two collages I had made as gifts: one with a small map of Kentucky in the center, surrounded by photos of her life from infancy through marriage, including siblings and their little white country church; the other of her new life, including her and Mr. B. as king and queen of Mardi Gras.

After a date, Mother's approach would be announced by laughter and merriment from those who called to her. She'd roll in, talking nonstop about where she and Mr. B. had been.

"People just go on about us two old coots falling in love, and they think it's wonderful that we've got each other," Mother chirped. "I'm just as happy as if I had my right mind."

They were attending nearly every function offered: parties, church, singings, bowling, exercise classes, games of horseshoe and beanbag throwing, and too many other fun things to name. The activities directors work hard to stay ahead of the residents!

Mr. B. was able to go along with a group that bowled in the public bowling lanes, but he and Mother missed each other so badly when apart that he didn't take advantage of the other numerous outings such as shopping, eating in restaurants, and sight-seeing. The relief on his face

was very evident when he'd spot Mother upon his return—and her thumbnail clicking would end.

"He says he doesn't know how he can stand it if something happens to me, that he's waited all his life to find his
'little jewel,'" Mother said as her eyes twinkled. "I feel the
same about him, but I do keep preparing myself in case he
does have that disease."

Every minute was precious to them both, and they sat
for hours hand in hand, just enjoying each other's company. Months passed, and Mr. B.'s health seemed so good
that even I wondered if the diagnosis had been correct. But
eventually faint clouds began to gather in their sunny
skies.

14

Sunshine and Shadow with Mr. B.

I WAS SO IN HOPES THE DOCTORS WERE WRONG," Mother wrote, and I knew what was coming. "Today was the first sign I've seen of any sickness, and I've just felt hurt all day.

"He was coming to my room to get me and smiling so big. But instead of turning in, he kept on going. He stopped smiling and looked puzzled but just walked on by. An aide heard me calling to him and brought him back. He said he could see me but couldn't get to me."

Weeks passed before another episode, and Mother pacified herself that perhaps he'd just awakened and was still half asleep.

We were so blessed. Before his symptoms really got bad, we enjoyed three wonderful Christmases at the house. Yes, they got their "two good years"—and then some!

Mother wanted Mr. B. to taste her baking at least once, so she saved her crochet money to buy ingredients for a fruitcake. (I never told her how much that cake *really* cost at today's prices, as she wanted so badly for it to be from her.) I took her home prior to the holiday, but she didn't have strength to stir the heavy mix. So I gave her enough easy things to do that she laughingly said that maybe she could take a "smidgen" of the credit. Back to the nursing home she went with a big piece of fruitcake for him and little samples for other friends. Her mind was at ease—she'd *baked* for him.

Sometimes holidays are celebrated early at the nursing home so family members with other plans can still visit their loved ones and enjoy the meal together, or residents "going out" can eat first with their in-home friends.

Prior to her courtship with Mr. B., Mother usually wanted me to fry catfish for Christmas dinner. Now she launched out, and I took their requests in advance each year. Once it was chicken baked with carrots, potatoes, and celery over a bed of rice along with giblet gravy. Another time it was ham, green beans, sweet potato patties, and hot rolls. Desserts were pumpkin pie, pumpkin bread, or cherry pie served with a little whipped topping or ice cream. How delightfully surprised Mother was when I prepared a chestnut dressing so common in her childhood days! Because we didn't live in chestnut country, she'd not eaten them for many years. These were a gift to us from out of state.

Seasoning was kept very light so Mama and Mr. B. wouldn't join other residents with postholiday upset stomachs. They both ate heartily (to state it mildly) and wrapped food to take for snacking and sharing.

For each of those three precious Christmases, after our meal we moved into the den, where Mother's crocheted ornaments hung from the little aluminum tree, and craft items from friends decorated walls and furniture. Jacklyn would join us for the holiday and read the Christmas story. We all sang the carols of Mother's and Mr. B.'s choice, always ending with "Amazing Grace" and prayer.

Then we would distribute gifts—lots and lots of little gifts. I learned after Mother's first Christmas in the nursing home not to purchase "big" gifts. She had tried hard to cover her disappointment as she opened packages revealing a warm sweater, scarf, and coat.

"That's nice; thank you very much, Honey; hang them in my closet," she commented.

Later, when a friend had wheeled in to see Mother's presents, she couldn't believe they were put away already.

"Mrs. Martin, get those things out, and put that sweater on!"

"It's too hot a day—I'll burn up," she returned.

"Well, look at all the rest of us. We're sweating up a storm, but we wouldn't miss showing off our new presents for anything. Put it on!" She wheeled out with a wink.

From that experience I learned to buy little gifts for Mother and Mr. B. What fun they had opening package after package to find stamps, a film container or medicine bottle stacked with quarters for the cold drink machine, postal cards, notebook paper, envelopes, pens, pencils, hairpins, Scotch tape, glue, batteries for the keyboard and cassette player, balls of crochet thread, skeins of yarn, stockings, socks, orange slices, T-shirts, cotton slips, Bible quiz cards, puzzle books, a belt, slippers, gingersnaps, and thumbtacks for their bulletin boards. Even a new dress never received the attention of those little things that were exclaimed over and shared.

"Thank you so much," they'd both say. "This has been the best Christmas yet."

When my photographs returned, showing the happy couple enjoying their holidays, I had plenty of duplicates for Mother to use to keep relatives and friends abreast of her courtship. But what the pictures didn't show on our last Christmas with Mr. B. was his slowness to open his gifts, as if he couldn't quite figure out why he was to tear the wrapping paper. The day passed without mishap, but we knew we were on a countdown with Alzheimer's.

Mother and Mr. B. continued to attend all nursing home gatherings, sitting together lost in their own world. But more and more often aides brought him to her after finding him wandering around looking for her. When the two said good-night, Mother would escort *him* to his room and wait outside the door until he was oriented to the surroundings.

More weeks passed, and Mother would dream, "Well, if he doesn't get any worse than that, I can take care of him."

Gently I admonished, "But he *will* get worse, Mama. This is just the beginning."

"He's doing so well—I wonder if we couldn't get married and live in the nursing home together so I can take care of him," I began to hear.

"Mama, when he gets bad, he'll not even know you're in the same room," I discouraged. "I wish there was some way you could marry, but we've seen enough symptoms now to know what's coming, even if he doesn't."

Soon it was "You were right, Kathryn Joyce. Today he had his shoes on the wrong feet and one day came out in his socks."

Mother had controlled nearly everything in her life, but now she battled his Alzheimer's—the first thing she'd come up against that wouldn't bow down.

It was pathetic to watch her struggle. In between symptoms Mr. B. was still a "fun" man, and Mother fought frantically to make life stay the same. They still shared a daily soda from the machine Mother learned to operate when she first learned he liked soft drinks. But now she had to assist him in holding his glass. He tired more easily, so they sat longer in the TV area—where Mother *still* didn't watch but sometimes "heard the best program when Oprah interviewed a retired one-room schoolteacher."

Mother stayed on the lookout for used clothing for Mr. B. to help keep him looking nice. When his legs began to weaken, Mother knew someone who donated a wheelchair. She was at ease about his spiritual condition, because he asked the Lord to come into his heart one day as they prayed together, and later he testified to it in one of the church services.

"I'm glad you didn't encourage me to marry," she would admit occasionally when the bad times started. "You were right. I couldn't have managed him. He starts out walking, and he just goes around in circles. It's pitiful. He can't remember to eat, so I've gotten permission to sit with him and help him. One lady tells me I don't have to fool with him—that's why the aides are here, and why don't I get on with my life? But I told her, 'I love him, and as long as God gives me strength, I'll take care of him.'"

"I'm sorry I'm so much trouble," Mr. B. apologized.

"Oh, Honey, you're no trouble—I love you, and I love doing for you," she assured with a pat.

"How long have we been married?" he asked, then realizing, answered, "Oh, we're *not* married, are we?"

He was forgetting how to use a spoon and was dropping his food, so Mother sewed together some bibs and began feeding him. Although he grew quieter, he still did well at bowling and attended events with Mother, their wheelchairs side by side.

He began to take longer naps throughout the day, and Mother, lost without him, began throwing herself with a frenzy into her nursing home activities.

15

"I Want to Do It All"

COME SEE WHAT I GOT YOU." Mother happily displayed a maroon T-shirt that read, "Treat Yourself—Visit a Nursing Home Resident Today."

"I won it for you in the talent show," she went on. "That makes three years I've entered, and I've played a different instrument each time—the piano, the accordion, and my harmonica."

"Yes, and you've won something each time," I bragged. "I'm so proud of you—a first, second, and third place. But I'd have been proud if you hadn't won anything—just that you entered. I'll wear this T-shirt tomorrow." I thanked her.

She loved the talent shows so much that once she was taken straight from the ambulance, after a hospital stay with pneumonia, to participate and win on her way to her bed.

"You know, Kathryn Joyce, I feel as if I'm useful in here. Before, I never got called on for anything and just sat warming a seat. But here I'm needed, and people look as if they love me. Somebody warned me I was working too hard, helping with the music, tending to him, and delivering the mail. They said I must be getting paid. I said, 'If you mean money, no. But if you could see the looks on the faces of the people when I deliver the mail, you'd see that's pay enough.' They look forward to my coming, and I chat a minute or maybe adjust something for them. Some can't see to read and ask me if I'll read their mail to them. They just thank me and thank me and clutch their mail to their hearts when I hand it back.

"Some of the workers will call out to me, 'Did you bring my check today, Mrs. Martin?' just grinning because they don't even get their mail here, and I go along with them and say, 'Not today—you must not have paid your bills, and they've garnisheed your wages!'

"Then there are a few that never get any mail from anybody, and they just watch so hopeful. It's so sad. You know, I'm so fortunate. I get so much mail from all over. Sometimes I tear off the address labels from one of mine, like *Guideposts,* after I've finished reading it, and deliver it to them. And sometimes when I'm given a gift of little greeting cards, I address some to them and deliver it just like it is real mail. Some of them don't know any difference, and they are all so thrilled."

The mail route took the better part of an hour and covered quite a territory. But some of those who were bedfast asked her to come back and play music for them. Before her nursing home experience, I bought Christmas and birthday gifts of musical instruments: an Autoharp, a harmonica, and a keyboard. With these smaller instruments she was ready to travel. Also on the mail route she learned the interests of various residents and shared craft and crochet patterns on her return visits.

She volunteered to write letters for those who couldn't. During the Persian Gulf War, the activities director suggested writing to the troops. Stamps, paper, and envelopes were provided. Not only did Mother meet regularly with those who prayed for our military, but also she plunged into writing those serving in the gulf who were from the surrounding area.

"We'll be having a meeting on letter writing for those who haven't written yet and need a little help," the director announced, laughing. "Except for you, Mrs. Martin—you don't need any help."

Mother had already written 30 people! Many of the recipients wrote back, and 2 from close by even came to meet the 89-year-old when they returned home.

"There's just so much to do in here—and I want to do it all!" was her motto.

She continued to "play bowling," although she felt guilty at first when she had to start playing without Mr. B. For a while he wanted to bowl so badly he'd be helped from his chair and held up to participate. Later he bowled from his wheelchair, but all too soon he couldn't remember anything about the game and went just to be with Mother.

When he could walk, he gripped her wheelchair so he wouldn't get lost on the way to meals or afternoon coffee and cookies. When he became wheelchair bound, he rolled along behind her. But the sad day arrived when he was unable to follow. Aides wheeled him to his dates. He paid attention but couldn't take part in activities. He sat secured in the wheelchair so he wouldn't fall out, or he lay in his room asleep.

He could still talk at times, although in between clear thinking he'd suddenly ask Mother to get his tools out of the wheelbarrow or to be sure and lock the gate. Her heart would nearly break.

She faithfully began going to his room when he was moved to the skilled care area, feeding him his three meals a day and balancing coffee and cookies down the hall to him at snack time.

When he was rolled out into the TV area for his programs, Mother joined him. From the light in his eyes we knew he recognized her, although he couldn't always call her name. Sometimes he asked about her daughter.

They sat side by side, hand in hand. If he was looking at television or dozing, Mother worked puzzles or crocheted, watching over him.

As he became bedfast, sleeping nearly all the time, Mother checked on him frequently. Other friends now looked in on him to help her. Sometimes she sat quietly by his bed if he was restless, just to assure him she was there. Some nights an aide came to her room to get her to help settle him down, because he occasionally fought those who readied him for bed.

"I wish I could be in the same room with him [I couldn't believe my mother said that!] so he wouldn't get scared when he doesn't recognize the aides and thinks it's somebody bad trying to kill him. But the social services lady said it wouldn't look right even at our ages and him helpless."

Trying to be all things to all people by filling needs for others, Mother occasionally gave up and stayed in bed herself.

"You know Mrs. Martin's sick when she doesn't come out of that bed," aides and nurses said. In fact, her illnesses now came mostly from that same old independent streak of which she was so proud—she just wouldn't take it easy. She really was trying to do it all.

16

Collector's Paradise, Daughter's Distress

M AMA, WE'RE GOING TO HAVE TO DO SOMETHING about this room," I said as I shook my head in wonderment.

"Now, Kathryn Joyce, you just stay out of my things— I've got them just as I want them!" was the response.

"Mother [I used the formal word to mean business], the health department is going to come after you!"

Unlike the neat house she'd kept in earlier years, her half of the room was a mess. She was "too busy" to fool with it.

In addition to keeping her own belongings, she was keeping so many possessions for others that another chest of drawers was brought in. She saved every little cut-and-paste gift any child made for her, every gift of craft or whatnots anyone brought, every empty jar she could find to give back to those who brought jellies, every Sunday School paper or tract she could pass on to whoever had a need, every single—well, you get the idea.

Although she could ask for coffee at any time, she kept instant coffee of her own. Most fruit was shared with friends, but apples were for her sweetheart. She saved them to scrape into applesauce to feed Mr. B., who could no longer chew well. Everything was so unorganized that she had to root and dig through the disorder to find things.

"I don't know how it gets like this," I fussed. "I just helped you clean up a few weeks ago."

When she gave permission to throw away just plain litter, we'd tidy up again.

One day Dot gestured to me after Mother had had enough and rolled out of the room during a cleaning session.

"Kathryn, I hate to tell on her, but I also hate to see you working so hard. The reason you have so much to keep throwing away"—she peeked to see if Mother had turned back —"is that you no sooner get out of sight than your mama goes into our trash cans and gets most of the stuff out and puts it back."

No wonder it all looked familiar! I started taking trash to cans throughout the corridors.

Keeping things was bad enough, but then Mother started *collecting.*

"Kathryn Joyce, did you know you can make money saving pop cans?" She was thrilled. "I can make some extra money, and that will help you."

"Mama, you can't save cans in a nursing home," I said into the phone by long distance.

"I've already started," she announced, "and the residents are saving theirs for me too. They bring them to me, and I rinse them out. When you come in from speaking, you can take them and get the money."

Sure enough, visitors could hardly finish their drinks before some resident pounced and said, "May I have that can when you're through? Mrs. Martin saves them."

When I came in the next time, I just stood in the doorway and stared. Every available inch was taken by boxes— all filled with aluminum cans! Dot shook her head and grinned.

The rule was "No boxes on the floor," and Mother had evaded that by one inch; the frame of the hospital-type table let one box rest an inch above the floor. The wardrobe tops had boxes. The folding chair had boxes. The chests of drawers had boxes. Mother, innocent in her nap, looked dwarfed by them. In fact, the boxes were so big and so packed with cans, some of which she'd managed to crush, that I could fit only one at a time atop her wheelchair to roll out to the van. And that day the closest I was able to park was a block away. Someone felt sorry for me and brought in a big flatbed dolly from maintenance to help.

When I came back with only $17.34, I thought that would be discouraging enough for her to quit. But, *no*— she'd been in the nursing home so long that $17.34 sounded like a lot of money, so it just *encouraged* her. And when riding my bike in the early mornings, I found myself swinging off to pick up cans. In front of my former English teacher's beautiful home I worked extrafast, hoping she (who had held such big hopes for me) wouldn't see me down in the ditch fishing out a can. Fortunately, Mother tired of this collection after a few hauls and moved on to something else.

"You know, Kathryn Joyce [those words could really do wonders to tighten tummy muscles], they always bring us a couple of little packets of seasoning with our meals. Well, Dot and I neither one care for it, and they throw them in the trash when they pick up our trays, so we're saving them for you. We already have 75."

When some of her friends found out she was saving the seasoning packets, they stopped the kitchen help from throwing theirs away too and brought them to Mother.

And each letter or call contained the weekly reports: "Made three more little 'squeeze my cheeks and I'll give you a kiss' things"; "Made 39 playing bowling"; "Have 221 little packets of 'false salt and pepper' things" . . .

Made of dried herbs, garlic, onion, and pepper, the "false salt and pepper" made a delicious seasoning in my cooking, and that made Mother happy. The nursing home eventually realized how little was actually being used by residents and made some changes. But nearly four years after the "false salt and pepper" phase—well, I still won't have to buy any for a long time.

Added to all the collecting, crocheting, craft making, and Mr. B. tending, Mother was asked to play music for more groups. Her playing was with the rhythm of her childhood, so the groups just adjusted and sang her way.

"I play for some 12 services a month now," she said as a sense of importance filled her voice. "Sometimes I go down at night when it's all empty on that side and practice. Some of the old songs I've wanted to learn have come to me, like 'I'm Going That Way,' 'Red Wing,' 'My Wild Irish Rose' . . .

"Now and then somebody will come over into the dining room and sit and listen and request. A couple of people have tried to get me to take money for playing, but I tell them I just enjoy it. They seem to like singing along."

She was into so many things that every time I thought I was nearing the end of what started to be a small booklet, I had to add another chapter!

17

Green Thumb and Grit

"KATHRYN JOYCE, YOU REMEMBER you said they'll let folks in here have a garden if they want?" Mother prompted. "Well, I've met the nicest lady who likes gardening the way I do and says that's what she misses most of all. She's 90 and one of those people that can't be still, always has to be doing something—kind of nervous energy. I thought a garden would be the very thing to help her. So I asked, and, sure enough, they said we can have a garden right out back in the little fenced-in yard! She's so excited."

"Wonderful, Mama!" I encouraged. "Just be careful not to fall."

Maintenance employees worked the ground for them, and Mother contacted friends, who, along with staff members, brought in gifts of seeds and fertilizer. I recall thinking, "I bet my mother is the only one in a nursing home who gets manure for a present—and is thrilled with it at that!"

Mother's room was already crowded with plants as gifts from her visitors. Some residents were bringing their plants to Mother to "resurrect" for them or to keep herself. Often their guests were brought to see the display of flowers and given a cutting along with directions for care. Further trips to visit loved ones would include giving a cutting to Mother from their own gardens.

When she moved into the nursing home, Mama realized she didn't have the strength to work a garden from her wheelchair or even a lower stool outside, so she simply began working her own personal "greenhouse" inside. I've seen everything in her room from Christmas cactus to Easter lily, begonia to poinsettia, "ivory" vine to portulaca moss, and a bunch I can't name.

Anyone on staff receiving a burn would head for Mrs. Martin and her aloe vera plant. She'd break off a piece and doctor them with its healing juice.

When I'd go over early (6:30 A.M. was about the only time I was fairly well assured to catch her for a visit), I'd push her out along the sidewalks between the nursing home and hospital. Way out back there were trees and a lawn with a picnic table, where I could sit. En route there were hundreds of flowers blooming in barrels, and one time Mother yelled, "Whoa! Stop! Wait a minute—let me get a cutting!"

"Mama, we can't pinch off the hospital's flowers. Somebody will think we're stealing." I glanced around nervously.

"Kathryn Joyce, it's not stealing a bit more than the man on the moon! They've planted their seed too close together, and the flowers need to be thinned out. They're not healthy." She stated it seriously, annoyed that I couldn't realize this on my own.

And I could just see the headlines: "Local Woman Turned Speaker Turns Flower Thief" or "Flower Thievery Ring Unearthed at Local Nursing Home."

But she was right. The plants looked healthier after she'd thinned them, and her little cuttings turned into full-grown flowers themselves.

And what gardens the two ladies had—healthy green plants with beautiful red tomatoes, shiny black eggplants, peas, okra, corn, mustard greens, and peppers, to name a few.

"The aide forgot to turn the alarm off the other day when I went outside with my friend to see how things were coming along in our garden; and when we opened that door, that big buzzer went off, and nurses and aides came running from every direction. I said, 'Uh-oh—we were too slow making our escape, and now you've caught us!' Did they laugh!" She chuckled each time she told the story.

"A nurse cooked our peas in the microwave for us" and "One of the staff is taking some of our crop home to cook and bring back" were other accounts. I was kept abreast of nearly every leaf on every plant and how good their produce tasted.

For years Mother had sought to find what in her childhood was called a "dishrag" gourd—a fibrous, somewhat spongy gourd. In a garden store I found a counter with packets of "Crazy Seeds," somewhat offbeat items grown for fun. Sure enough, there was the gourd used for dishwashing and scrubbing in the early 1900s. But now it is the famous and expensive "loofah," sold as a beauty aid.

Mother had previously harvested a bumper crop at home and saved the seeds. I took them over, and she dropped them into the rich, black soil. If I thought she had had a bumper crop at her own garden, I hadn't seen anything to compare with the vines and gourds that took over the hurricane fence out back of the nursing home!

She offered to split the proceeds with the maintenance man if he'd get a local store to market them, but he was timid about asking. So she peeled, deseeded, and halved them with him and gave the rest for gifts—and gave the rest for gifts—and gave the rest for gifts! I shall never have to buy a loofah as long as I live!

"I'm just as proud of our gardening as I can be, and it's done wonders for my friend; but the one thing I can't seem to grow is a rosa montana," Mother often fretted.

My father had used an arbor to support the weight and beauty of his many beautiful rosa montanas with their pale green, leafy vines and tiny, delicate, heart-shaped pink flowers. But it was the one plant that Mother's green thumb failed to grow.

"Well, this little montana didn't make it either." Her disappointment was evident each time another died.

The only one to show signs of life was accidentally mowed down.

"I wondered why one of the maintenance men wouldn't look up when he passed my window," she wrote. "He usually taps on the glass and cuts up with me. Somebody told me he killed my montana and is afraid to face me. So I called him in and told him not to worry—if that's the biggest thing to go wrong in my life, I'll be happy."

So she tried again. I covered the struggling little plant with pine straw in the cooler months, and she even dug it up and took it inside during the few weeks of really cold winter.

Other than the rosa montana, everything she planted grew, and she touched the lives of many with still another name: "the gardening lady."

18

Party Time

THE YEARS CONTINUED TO HURRY BY, and so did Mama. She'd chalked up 90 birthdays, so we had a party! It was hard to schedule the surprise, because her day was already full. She would be eating her own meal, feeding Mr. B. each meal plus a snack, playing the piano for a morning function, delivering the mail, and lying down to rest between each engagement. So I had to set the party at the only time open: between bingo and supper. That's right—*bingo!* All those years she had refused even to look toward the dining area when bingo was played.

"I just don't think I'd feel right about it," she confided to me each time she was invited to join in the game.

But someone explained the playing to her and that there was no gambling, only prizes for winners. So off she went out of politeness and the challenge.

"Why, it's just like you said about playing bowling: It's a nice game that's been taken to the wrong places and got a bad name," further qualifying, "It's not as if you have to put money 'up front.'" (*I* didn't even know that term!)

Now she was a regular, keeping me up-to-date on what she had won—baby powder, a hand mirror, $3.00, $2.00, and other nice little gifts furnished by organizations who wanted to do something for the residents. So with this latest activity added, there was only one open hour even to *consider* scheduling a party!

I arrived early that day and tied a balloon to her chair to float and announce, "I'm 90 today." She had been made over since early morning. As her guests slipped through the big dining room en route to the small one, they were unnoticed by Mother, so intent was she on her bingo game.

Friends from both outside and inside the nursing home helped decorate and prepared to serve. The nursing home supplied the punch, and another friend supplied homemade candy. The cake I ordered said "Happy 90th Birthday" and was decorated with a mailbox and a treble clef. The aroma of floral gifts and sounds of excitement filled the room. We waited for Mother.

Bingo over, she had already rolled back to her room before we could catch her. On the pretense of having coffee, Spencer and Lillian brought her back.

Laughing with them, she was well into the room and speaking to each person when she suddenly realized that everyone in there was a personal friend, whether new or from years back. And they were all there for her, singing "Happy Birthday."

She was overwhelmed from the joy of it, and tears glistened in her eyes. I too was touched at the efforts visitors had made to come, for I knew several of them had physical problems of their own.

The guests ranged in age from 20-something to 90-something. Those who couldn't attend that Friday afternoon continued to stop by throughout the evening and the whole weekend. Gifts, cards, and calls poured in as well.

People who had been in my audiences and other friends Mother never met thought to remember special days with cards and gifts, and that day was no exception. After we'd wheeled her back to her room, I presented one such gift from a friend in the Memphis church. Mother's expression was of pure consternation as she opened Dorothy's present. It looked like a thick paper pad or receipt book. It was a book of brand-new $1.00 bills, 90 of them—one for each year of her life! Dorothy's own mother had received it as a gift but was too ill to spend it in her final days. Dorothy wanted it to be enjoyed.

"Are they real?" Mama whispered as she thumbed through the "pages."

I assured her they were.

She began to count aloud, silent only as she inhaled: "One, 2, 3, 4, 5, 6, 7-8-9-10," as she ran out of breath, "14, 15, 16, 17, 18-19-20-21," wheeze, "27 . . ." all the way to 90, completely oblivious to all the sounds of enjoyment we were making as we watched her.

That birthday was the biggest celebration she'd ever had, and when she had rested up from it all, she plunged into her 91st year with renewed vigor.

19

Keeps Right on Going

"YOU WENT *WHERE*, MAMA?" Surely I had heard wrong.

"I said I went to the circus," she answered.

"The *circus*? You went to the *circus*?" I repeated incredulously.

Ninety years old, and she had gone to her first circus! All those years she had abided by her church rules, and they stated in black and white no circus attendance!

"The nursing home was taking a van load the other night and had an empty seat, so I decided to go. You know, with him sleeping so much, I knew he wouldn't miss me and worry. I tell you, it was more fun! My favorite part was the little dogs performing tricks. If they weren't the cutest things!"

Her smile turned to disgust. "I didn't approve of the way those women dressed that did the trapeze, though. You can't tell me it's necessary to go out in public with so little on!"

Happiness flooded her face again. "But everything else was so enjoyable. I didn't think there was any harm to going, especially when I saw how many people brought their little children. So I thought once wouldn't hurt me, and nobody'd ever have to know I'd been. But, lo and behold, when we left early so we wouldn't get knocked down, who should I meet face-to-face in the aisle but Wylie!" (A young man from her church)

"Oh, oh!" she had burst out laughing when she saw him. "Be sure your sins will find you out! You'd better not tell on me, Wylie!" Then she quickly added, "I wish I'd said, 'I won't tell on *you* if you won't tell on *me!*'" And she rocked with mirth.

With other residents going out for such treats on a regular basis as well as overnight stays, I felt bad that Mother didn't go out more often.

"I'm really content to stay right here," she usually answered my invitations. "It's too tiring on me to go, and to tell you the truth, I guess I'm afraid I'll miss something in here!"

But every long once in a while, off we went. To take her in and out of a vehicle was hard on both of us, so for "people visits" I just pulled into driveways, and friends came out to chat at the window. They were always surprised at her recall of the names of their family members and her interest in each one. Some even asked me privately, "Why is your mother in the nursing home? There's nothing wrong with her." And I said, "It's *because* she's in the nursing home there's 'nothing wrong' with her!"

For a "store visit" she had strength for only one store on an outing, and I'd take the wheelchair for that. She was a lot more interested in *whom* she saw in the aisles than *what* she saw on the shelves; she enjoyed meeting new people. We never failed to hear, "There's the mail lady!" or "There's the music lady!"

With her favorite store located in the next city, she'd visited there; but, except to vote at City Hall, she had not seen the major changes in our own city. For years the downtown area had been nearly deserted. The unused depot had shown its age, having been rebuilt only after the original was burned during the Civil War. Most store buildings had been closed, their windows dusty and forlorn.

Then someone got the idea of its becoming an "antique city." Flower beds were planted here and there along the sidewalks. United States flags became conspicuous throughout the business area and on many homes. The depot was restored and renamed The Country Market. It houses local crafts, jellies, candies, and such. A mail car from the railroad's heyday was pulled alongside, half of it just as it was while in service, complete with mailbags and pigeonholes for sorting letters. The other half houses one of several art galleries.

Historians traced paint colors, and each building on the main street was repainted as closely as possible to its original color. Most are dedicated entirely to antiques—not junk or just used items, but first-rate-quality items, from tiny toys to massive furniture. Once-empty sidewalks are bustling as tourists arrive by car and busloads to shop or browse. Nice bed-and-breakfast facilities have opened. Even our town mascot, Old Hardhide, the alligator (who has his own newspaper column), receives many visitors each day.

I wanted Mother to see the changes up close. Finally one hot Friday she decided to let me take her around one block. As I pushed her along, the conversation went like this:

"Oh, Kathryn Joyce, look at those old button shoes in the window. I wore some like that as a girl. I hope I don't miss the lady who teaches Sunday School on Sunday mornings. This is the day she usually comes to my room, and we go over the Scriptures together. Well, look at that coal oil lamp. I used one like that sometimes long after I had electricity, just for the memories. Myrtle said she'd keep an eye on him, and if I don't get back in time, she will deliver the mail. Oh, here's a little baby doll from way back. One of my friends has started carrying a baby doll. I guess she thinks she's a little girl again. Look at those cedar wardrobes—how beautiful the wood is! I keep his clothes in my wardrobe in my room. I hope he's OK. Poor darling—he hardly knows he's in the world some days and reaches out like he's throwing something. I try not to dwell on it—it hurts me so bad."

Perspiration turned to sweat as I pushed her along, stopping now and then to pull backward over an uneven sidewalk. Her 169 pounds plus the weight of the chair weren't helping.

"I just don't know why you're puffing and sweating so, Kathryn Joyce," she paused long enough in her nonstop chatting to observe. "I'm not a bit hot."

"I guess you're not," I grunted between gasps. "You're not pushing around 200 pounds in 95-degree weather either!"

She laughed. "Well, I guess you *do* have a point there."

As on other outings, she was soon eager to get back. It was as if the nursing home couldn't run itself with her away. And sometimes I wondered if it could!

The kitchen staff had been notified that she wouldn't be back for lunch, so I ordered one of our town's delicious specialties, a fried oyster "Po-Boy." With the van parked in the shade of a tree, we faced the depot as we divided the big French-bread sandwich. We were entertained by the crowds passing under the huge American flag, up so high it could be seen for miles.

As we sat observing the typical downtown scene, I felt good about being able to show Mama what improvements had been made in the area. Then she proceeded to tell me more about each remodeling in town than I knew! She'd kept up with everything by reading the news accounts as they happened, for she also delivered all the area *newspapers* in addition to the mail!

I returned her to the nursing home, where she checked on Mr. B., rested a bit, and got back to "busyness." And I went home, where I collapsed for the rest of the day.

20

Blessing and Blessings

I BELIEVE I'M STARTING TO SLOW UP, Kathryn Joyce." Mother broached the forbidden subject one day when I caught her lying down.

"I sure can't tell it from where I stand." I grinned.

"Well, I can't hold out as long as I did—have to rest longer, and some days I just feel worn out and stay in bed."

"You try to do too much," I cautioned. "Just ease up a little." My glance around the room took in the uneven letters of her name on the wheelchair—"CECILE" instead of "CECIL."

"Mama! Who took it on themselves to add an *E* to your name?" I griped. It had always been so frustrating to make corrections on nearly every piece of business mail, explaining she's "Cecil" and not "Cecile." But what audacity for someone to mark her personal property!

"Oh, *I* did that," she explained. "All my life people have misspelled my name; and I've got so tired of correcting them that I figured I can't win, so I might as well give in and misspell it just like the rest of them! Oh, yes, while you're here, I've got you a bag of persimmons in the refrigerator. Be sure and have the nurse get them."

Being so friendly and helpful to everyone, Mother quite often received gifts of foods that we liked but couldn't get. Those little persimmons were from a man who came to the nursing home three times a day to feed his wife.

"He's always picking at me," she said, chuckling. "Says he's got plenty more but can't reach them, so one

106

day he's going to put me up in his tree so I can shake them down."

I retrieved the large bag of persimmons and feasted while seated in the wheelchair with my feet propped on Mother's bed frame.

"The Lord sure has been good about providing for us, hasn't He?" she remarked.

"He sure has," I agreed. "I'm planning to write a book about that someday after I finish my book about you."

"Whatever can you find to say about me that's taking you so long to write it?" she pondered naively.

"Well, you keep on getting into things that will be interesting and helpful to other people, so I keep on trying to keep up with you," I joked.

"I just want my life to count for something," she said seriously. "Sometimes I sing that song 'Will There Be Any Stars in My Crown?' and I ask the Lord to make me a blessing. I testify to how God has helped me, how sick I was and yet went home for several years, and how full my life is in here. Some listen, some don't, but you can't win people by preaching to them—you have to live it. They listen more to your life than your words."

And what an assortment of listeners!

"There are so many wonderful people in here. Some outsiders just don't realize how entertaining some of these folks are. When I deliver the mail and get invited back to chat, I ask the aides to watch him while I go visit. I don't crochet on Sundays, so that's when I go calling on those who can't come to services. It's so interesting to hear them tell about themselves. There's a university professor, and he's told me about his experiences earning his degrees and teaching. One fellow fished and trapped in the swamps all his life, and his stories are intriguing. A blind man I know still gets called on to recane chairs. Very few know that trade anymore. One lady can't talk since her stroke. But when her husband died, I went and sat with her awhile. She just held on to my hand. She thinks a lot of you, and I can tell when she asks about you as she motions far off with her good hand. And I say, 'You're asking about Kathryn?' She'll nod and smile, and I tell her where you're speaking."

She leaned forward to speak confidentially. "You know, I think the same man who made a pass at me must have said something to her too, for I saw her bop him over the head with her pocketbook."

I burst out laughing. The picture of such an elegant lady "bopping" someone . . .

"You sure never had any more trouble out of him after you put him in his place, did you?" I snickered.

The man had waved Mother down one day in her hurry to meet Mr. B. Thinking he needed help, she stopped.

"He sidled up close to my wheelchair and put his hand on my leg," she had written. "I said, 'Here! What do you think you're doing?' and he said, 'I just want to get in on the action.'

"I told him, 'I'm a Christian lady, and we don't carry on like that—and if we did, it wouldn't be any of *your* business; and if you ever put a hand on me again, you'll draw back a nub!'"

"He just nods politely now when I go past," she demonstrated with a curt nod and sour expression. "But back to what I was talking about, the Lord providing," she retraced, "how I prayed when I needed new teeth and found out the state would help."

The nursing home had worked together with her on setting up schedules with both the dentist and the company that transports residents for such appointments. She had rejoiced when notified of approval and made the subsequent visits. She came away all smiles with the new teeth.

"I've heard so many complain about new teeth and

how hard it is to get used to them when you're up in age. But I had already made up my mind before I ever went that I was going to wear them." And she did.

"So thank the Lord we're all up-to-date on teeth and eyes," she added.

I reminisced with her about the eye checkup. In the reception area at the eye doctor's office, updating her records, I ran out of room trying to list her "hobbies and special interests" in the good-sized space allotted. After the exam we were told there wasn't enough change to warrant new glasses. She could see as well with or without her glasses, even for crocheting. She wore them only to keep her eyes from feeling tired.

Mama's casual approach to every crisis was "The Lord will make a way, for where there's a will, there's a way." I often teased, "Yes, Mama, but *I'm* the 'way' it usually happens!"

Very soon we were to experience God's help in another unexpected way.

21

Home at Last

EVERYBODY IS SO EXCITED about going to hear you speak," Mother announced. "I don't know how many I've talked to that say they're going. Even the nursing home is bringing a load."

"I sure hope so," I said, worried. "It'd really be embarrassing for nobody to show up—you know, a 'prophet in his own country' or *me* in *my own* hometown."

"Oh, they'll be there, all right," Mother assured me. "Folks ask about you all the time, and lots have seen you on the TV."

Mother had seen a small degree of my work in the early days and heard it on my album and tapes. The only television program I ever knew her to watch was one of my appearances on a national network.

Her neighbor had called her at 7 A.M. to come over, saying that she'd just seen a preview of "Miz Maudie" and "Kathryn" for a program about to air in a few minutes. (It was done live at prime time originally and recorded for later viewing in some parts of the country.)

"But Mama, how did you manage to wake up and get ready and get next door on your walker so quickly?" I had asked.

"Oh, I was already ready. I got up and dressed at 5:30 just in case."

"Aren't you afraid you'll get criticized for watching TV?" I followed up.

"You can't tell me that some who feel it's a sin—if it had been *their* child—you can't tell me they wouldn't have been sitting right there watching too!" she rationalized triumphantly.

So hopefully now there would be a good crowd, and Mother would come closer to seeing in person what I do. The local church hosting the special service had advertised it as an evening of entertainment and inspiration for the community.

"I've been feeling pretty bad, so I'm trying to rest more to be able to go hear you," she said from her rocker in the corner, an unusual sight.

I had just flown in from fall retreat speaking and was surprised to see how subdued Mother appeared. Even the room looked somewhat barren as she had sold or given away a number of items to "make it easier" on me.

The big night arrived, and the building was packed. The start was delayed while ushers brought out folding chairs to seat everyone. I was touched to see such a representation and learned later that many people could not get in, so they were hoping for another appearance.

And there on the front seat was Mother, absolutely beaming! She was a part of the tremendous roars of laughter and applause from the audience, although she was slightly feverish from pleurisy.

After "Miz Maudie" exited and I reappeared as myself, I endeavored to express my appreciation to the wonderful crowd, recognizing classmates, teachers, friends from childhood, patients from when I'd worked in a local dental office, and others. Nursing home residents shone as if I were their own. Even strangers who had come because of the advertising felt the warmth of welcome.

Last of all, I introduced my mother by asking her to wave so everyone could locate her, and I told briefly of her many hats at the nursing home. Upon dismissal, while I stood surrounded by people in the vestibule, greeting them individually, Mother was receiving her share of old acquaintances at her seat down front. On the way home she related what each had said.

The next few days she happily told me every comment that had been made to her about how my appearance had been enjoyed and appreciated for its clean humor with a message. But she just wasn't feeling any better and struggled to do her work—still feeding Mr. B., delivering the mail, and playing the piano for services.

"I've had to skip playing bowling and bingo the last few times," she admitted. "I think I'm going to have to give up some of the things I do. It's starting to tell on me now."

"Well, you're just two months from 91," I said, agreeing, "so you can do or not do whatever you want."

She placed her order for Christmas dinner, saying her appetite wasn't as big as before, so she didn't want much—just so there'd be enough for her to bring back to Mr. B., although he didn't know one day from another.

But friends offered to bring us an even better treat of fried turkey (made by immersing the whole turkey into an institutional-size container of hot vegetable oil), dressing, cookies and candies, and homemade pie. Mother expressed comfort in seeing that I had so many friends, a wonderful coworker who could stand in as a second mother, and work that I loved.

"Now I feel relieved that you'll be OK if something happens to me," she said as she prepared to enter the hospital to be treated for pneumonia.

On Christmas Day, instead of celebrating at the house, she was signing her wishes of not having life support in case it was needed.

"I'm so tired—I just want to go home," she said again and again.

She was referring to heaven, and in between the visits of the hundreds who came to see her, she sang the old songs that used to take up two pages in the hymnbooks.

After 10 days in the hospital, her allotted time to be gone from the nursing home expired, so I set about packing and moving her belongings back to the house. Myrna and I really hustled to cram everything into boxes and clear out even as the next family waited in the hall to move their loved one in. They just stood there looking somewhat dumbfounded about what was happening to them, and I thought, Welcome to the club.

Back and forth I went from home to hospital, leaving when Mother would fall asleep.

"I don't want you to grieve over me when I'm gone," she said in a hoarse voice, "for I've lived a long life, and I'm ready to go on now anytime. You've been a good daughter. I'm so proud of you and of the work you do for the Lord, encouraging people. Your daddy would be proud too if he could see how you've turned out.

"I hate to leave you and all my friends. Seems like these last few years in the nursing home I've enjoyed more than any."

Then she said these words, so simple and yet so deep, that were my theme and purpose during the writing of this book: *"I went to the nursing home to die, but instead I learned how to live."*

She continued, the sickness causing her to add the old "unhunhs" between sentences. "I feel God had a purpose for me being in there and that He's used me to help people in my own way. I've felt loved and appreciated by so many. Different ones will hug me or pat my arm and say they love me. You know, I told you a while back—my mother never told me she loved me. She was good to us children and saw to our needs, but I never recall her touching us or ever saying she loved us." (How sad to have carried that all those years!)

"I think it's like you said: she couldn't show what she'd never known. I'd just guess the relatives that took her in as an orphan really never wanted her and didn't show her any affection. She probably didn't know how."

Even that comfort could not bring back her strength, and she steadily weakened. Worse yet was the staph infection that now brought the "Isolation" sign to the door. She could do without food. She could do without playing bowling. She could even do without the piano. But she could not do without the steady influx of people. Still, I was surprised at the number who faithfully donned masks and gloves and came in anyway.

She was assured that Mr. B. was being checked on and the mail was being delivered, and, yes, it was harder than it looked—it was taking two people! And she was assured of all who had called or come by to ask about her or sent greetings, and those who made what score at bowling . . . She couldn't figure out how to use the phone but had hospital staff dial for her to check on those she was worried about—at all hours.

One morning an aide had put the TV on and left it. There was the one program I'd hoped Mother would one day get to see: *The Waltons.*

"Oh, Mama, there's that program I've told you about so many times! I know how you feel about TV, and I'll turn it off if you want. But if you won't feel bad about it, would you just glance to see what it's like?"

"Very well," she said agreeably. "Oh, Honey, look at that—they're at a quilting bee, sitting around a quilting frame just as we did in Kentucky!"

Actually the program was ending, and Earl Hamner was narrating the conclusion over the song "Seeing Nellie Home." But Mother and I sang along, "It was from Aunt Dinah's quilting party, I was seeing Nellie home."

The room resounded with Mother's croaky, hoarse voice as she relived happy memories of years past.

"Oh, Honey, I'm so glad I finally got to see that. It was wonderful! Thank you for telling me about it."

Thus I checked off another thing on my list I'd wanted to do for Mother.

*   *   *

"Did many people come to my funeral?"

"What funeral, Mama?" I urged.

"Didn't I die?"

"No, you came mighty close, but you're still here."

"But I saw Christ."

"Where, Mama?" I was eager to hear.

"Right there where you're standing, Honey."

"Did He say anything?" I asked.

Despite her sickness and great suffering, her face lit up, and she smiled radiantly. "No, He never said a word. He just stood there with His hands outstretched. I could see the scars so plain, as if He was beckoning me to come." And she launched into singing about growing homesick for heaven.

A young medical professional overheard and said, "She'll get better quicker if you can keep her from carrying on like that."

But after he left, a more experienced nurse who'd remained silent now spoke: "Don't try to hush her. I've been around longer than he has. If she said she saw Christ, then she saw Christ. I've witnessed too many critically ill at this point to ever dispute. This may not be her time to go, but many patients nearing the end have told me of seeing Christ. It's like He comes and takes the fear of death away to make passing easier."

When we were alone again, Mother wanted to talk about her funeral. I went over her simple plans but described some additions I wanted to make that would add some personal touches.

After this, Mother seemed to improve enough that I hurried back to Memphis to ready and pack for the winter's speaking. Within a few days I was at her side again, and she told me about the visitors she'd had, but now she was begging, pleading, even fussing that I would take her back to the nursing home.

"Kathryn Joyce, I want to go home to heaven, but I want to go to the nursing home first and see all my friends and make sure he's all right."

She had never fully understood about the staph infection and isolation, but, thank goodness, on that day the lab test finally showed clear, and she would be discharged.

Once again I met with social services in the hospital and nursing home. Because they'd both been watching her case and knew the circumstances, she was assigned a vacancy in the skilled care area, near the same room where she had started her first stay more than 11 years before.

Although she was no longer a resident of the nursing home, they had held on to her records and simply made corrections and updates with the parish, and I signed the papers.

I had already organized her belongings just in case and returned a lot less to the new room than I'd removed from the old one. When I'd put everything away and made the homey touches, I arranged for the ambulance to transport her from the hospital, next door, since she was virtually bedfast.

She could stand only if lifted by two therapists. Not realizing that she could no longer even sit up, she was secured to the bed or to the chair to keep her from trying to get up on her own and falling over.

Once back in the nursing home, she was disappointed that a miracle didn't occur immediately so that she could go see her friends. But word spread, and visitors from in the nursing home and out began to come, staying just a few minutes. It had been necessary to have the phone removed when we'd given up her old room, so people came in person.

Those who had been unable to see her were shocked by her extreme loss of weight and how she had aged. But they were thrilled to see that old light in her eyes and personal interest still in her voice.

She kept telling me that she would be all right, now that she was home, and wanted me to get on back to Memphis to fly out in a few days. Leaving town that next morning, I stopped for a last visit.

There in the TV area, secured in his wheelchair, was Mr. B.! For months he'd not seemed aware of anything, sleeping hour after hour. If awake, he just stared into space. But this morning he was alert, looking around, grinning and talking.

"Mr. B.!" I exclaimed happily. "It's so good to see you up! Did you know Mama is back?"

Such a crowd was gathered nearby that I couldn't hear his response, but I followed his nod and glanced over to his right.

There, hand in hand with him, sat Mama! She was tiny and frail, but her face was flushed with excitement as residents, staff, and outside visitors pushed their way to hug and kiss and welcome her back, teasing Mr. B. about his miraculous cure: "That love sure works wonders, doesn't it, Mr. B.?"

I managed to get close enough to exclaim over the both of them, kissing Mr. B. good-bye on the forehead. To Mother I gave a gentle hug, telling her there was such a crowd trying to get to her that I'd leave her to visit, and we'd make up for Christmas and her birthday on my next trip, when she was stronger.

She promised she'd try to eat and told me not to worry. With my kiss to her warm brow, I said, "I love you." And she answered with the words she'd learned to say only a few years before: "I love you too, Honey."

As I worked my way out of the press of friends, I

looked back one last time. Mother's face was aglow with joy—she was *home.*

That night, shortly after I arrived in Memphis and three hours before her 91st birthday, Mother got her final wish—she went home to heaven from her beloved nursing home.

22

Mama and the Funeral Home

IF I COULDN'T FINISH THIS BOOK during Mother's lifetime with her always "adding chapters," I don't know why I thought there could be a simple "The end" at her death. For there is nothing simple at all about her unending influence. I first became aware of its magnitude at the funeral.

Knowing that I would be too upset to think straight when the time came, we'd made and updated the plans again and again. With written instructions on file, there was no need for last-minute consulting with the nursing home, the funeral home, or the city cemetery officials. All was done according to wishes. From the "key contact people" lists I'd made, friends and relatives had notified others for me.

Because Mother was such an unconventional person, I wanted more than the traditional "insert-his/her-name" sermon she might get if the pastor from my childhood could not be reached. So we had agreed to have Jacklyn conduct our services. She had prepared long in advance in case of emergency.

We had planned with the funeral home for a week-night service if during a summer month, or a weekend day service if it was when darkness came early. Mother had me promise not to cancel an engagement if she died during speaking season, as "The Lord's work is more important, and I can wait." Thank God, it didn't have to be that way. With her death occurring on Friday night, Sunday afternoon was a perfect time for the community.

I had prepared myself for years but still fully expected to die myself, I hurt so badly. Even now, much later, finishing this last chapter is with tears. I can hardly wait for the part about the funeral, as it brings comfort every time I relive it.

With precious friends already present and at my side, I viewed the body. Could that be Mother? Was that how she had looked in earlier years? The only difference was her stillness, something I had never seen. For even in sleep she had been restless, as if eager to awaken and get involved in something else.

She was wearing her favorite old brown print dress, dubbed her "funeral dress," which she'd worn once weekly since I bought the material 17 years before. I'm sure funeral home personnel must have thought me stingy or poverty-stricken when it was brought to them with the soft old cotton undergarments and stockings Mother wanted.

Alongside the beautiful funeral sprays I placed other flowers people had purchased, intended as gifts for her birthday. To represent her gardening skills, I included one of her live amaryllis plants, with its four white blooms wide open.

Across front pews two afghans were displayed, the multi-colored one from her bed and the gray-blue one she'd made for me the previous Christmas. What I believed to be her masterpiece, a white popcorn-stitch crocheted bedspread, was draped across the beige casket, and in its center lay an unpretentious spray of roses.

Inside the casket with her, representing her music, lay her harmonica and kazoo. And between her fingers we placed her crochet needle, its hook still in the last stitch of the doily she'd begun. It was connected to the ball of thread inside her old clear plastic bowl with a feeder hole in the lid, which had kept the thread from tangling as it unrolled.

Everything in place, I realized how quiet the chapel was with the faint whispers of guests. Turning to face those who'd come early to help me, I said, "You know, if Mother could be rolling in from the back door instead of lying up here, she'd be laughing and calling out to you, 'What's everybody being so somber about? This is my *homegoing* we're celebrating!' So let's do everything the way Mother would want it."

There was nodding of agreement, and conversation resumed at a more natural volume, even interspersed with laughter as Mother's antics were recalled. New guests arriving looked surprised upon entry but soon caught on, and, all in good taste, it indeed became a celebration.

For a number of years I'd been concerned that because of her age and being out of circulation there'd be only a handful of people present. I need not have worried.

Along with the friends of years past, her life in the nursing home brought in new friends galore. If she'd been a prominent citizen active in business or social affairs, she could not have had more visitors. Except for one quick break just minutes before the service, I stood the entire three hours near the foot of the casket and continually greeted the long, never-ending lines.

If I'd felt proud of her before, it was nothing in comparison to the pride I felt now. And where I'd thought I would surely have a heart attack right on the spot, I found sweet consolation from each person.

Some fought to hold down laughter as they tried to tell me something Mother had told them not long before. Some wept. A successful young businessman who'd called Mother "Grandma Martin" since his childhood sobbed, "I already had her birthday card in my suit pocket to go see her." He had visited her regularly, made sure his children knew her, remembered her at birthdays and Christmastime, and even came in mask and gloves to see her in isolation. Now, as tears flowed, he opened his suit coat and showed me the card.

"Let's read it to her, OK?" I asked. I opened it and held it over her, reading the beautiful verses inside the card that read "From Your Grandson" on its cover. And we added it to her growing collection.

Another professional man wept, "Good-bye, you feisty ole biddy!" He choked. "You won't be planting any more gardens down here, so you won't need seed money. I'll give it to Kathy."

Hugging me, he quickly shoved an envelope with money into my hands and finished by sobbing, "I've gotta go cry now!" And too upset to stay, he left to cry in private.

Families of nursing home residents embraced me with their stories of what a help and encouragement Mother had been, not only to their loved ones, but also to them.

One young lady wiped tears as she said, "Your mama encouraged me to go back to school. I didn't think I could make it, but she said she didn't get her high school diploma until she was 57, and if she could do it, I could. And I did!"

Others from area churches told how she had played music for their services at the nursing home and what a blessing she had been to them—when *they* had gone intending to be a blessing to *her*.

Some, who had taken her tapes of their church services for her to borrow or books or patterns or gifts, I was able to thank face-to-face.

I was overwhelmed by those who came with their own recent hurts and losses, some who had stood just the day before where I was standing now.

"Dear God," I prayed silently, "I don't know how heaven works, but if at all possible, please let Mother see what's going on."

The crowd kept coming, and age, race, religion, social status—none of it mattered. I realized that was a big part of Mother's popularity. She never noticed any of those things. She saw only a person, a friend. She didn't have to adapt her ways or her conversation to fit anybody or any occasion. She was simply the same all the time. She was the one stable thing in the lives of many. If only everyone could be more like that!

As time for the service neared, folding chairs were brought out, and still there were people standing across the back and out into the lobby. Over the sound system came the music of my piano playing I had recorded months before, a medley of choruses from some of Mother's favorite songs: "My Old Kentucky Home," "My Home, Sweet Home," "The Unclouded Day," "There'll Be No Sorrow There," and "Sweet By-and-by."

Her new pastor, who along with his wife had visited Mother nearly every day since his arrival, read the obituary and the 23rd psalm and led in prayer. (Why didn't I think to include Mr. B. and her godchild as survivors?)

"When They Ring Those Golden Bells" was my last musical tribute before Jacklyn began her message, given to me afterward both on paper and audiocassette.

Cecil Martin Funeral Message
by Rev. Jacklyn Welch Shockley

Scripture Reading: Proverbs 31

I will not read all of this famous chapter, because I want to emphasize those portions of verses that contain the words "her hands."

v. 10: "Who can find a virtuous woman? for her price is far above rubies."

v. 13: "She . . . worketh willingly with *her hands.*"

v. 16: "With the fruit of *her hands* she planteth a vineyard."

v. 19: "She layeth *her hands* to the spindle, and *her hands* hold the distaff."

v. 20: "She stretcheth out *her hand* to the poor; yea, she reacheth forth *her hands* to the needy."

v. 30: "Favour is deceitful, and beauty is vain: but a woman that feareth the LORD, she shall be praised."

v. 31: "Give her of the fruit of *her hands*; and let her own works praise her in the gates" (emphases added).

Introduction

When my own mother died a few years ago, we went early for the family viewing before the wake.

She looked so different, so much younger and pain-free, it was hard to believe it was my mother. For the work of the funeral home staff and a beautician, plus the release of death, had erased the years of intense suffering and age.

Later my niece, who had been particularly close to Mama, said she had had fleeting doubts as to whether this was indeed her beloved "Nanny."

Suzanne thought, If I could only see her hands, I would know for sure this is truly my grandmother.

So while the rest of us were talking in another part of the room, she slipped over to the casket, and, lifting the little lacy handkerchief placed over those dear, familiar hands, she said, "Now I *know* that she is my Nanny."

We too can know by the hands that lie still before us who *this* is, for they are very special and distinctive hands. These hands, her hands, tell us a lot about the one who lies here and the life she has lived.

First of all, these were toiling hands.

Cecil Martin was reared on a farm in Webster County, Kentucky. Although the older brother and sister no longer lived at home, there was plenty of work for the four girls and one boy left. And Cecil often found herself toiling in the fields from sunup to sundown, six days a week.

Even though she moved to Louisiana after her

marriage, her roots were still in Kentucky—so much so that when her daughter, Kathryn, was in Kentucky a few years ago, she scooped up a little Webster County soil that will be mingled with the Louisiana soil as this transplanted Kentuckian is laid to rest.

As we have seen, this lady was no stranger to work. Not only did she teach in a one-room schoolhouse, but also she moved to Ponchatoula to raise strawberries, and the gentleman seated in front of me serving as pallbearer, George Gaten, was the young teenager who worked with her in her fields. After she'd left the farm, she continued to pack strawberries for other area farmers.

In addition to her housework, she worked as a chiropractor's assistant, an aide in an orphanage, a companion, and a sitter. During the Korean War she rolled bandages as a volunteer in New Orleans hospitals.

Like the woman in the Scripture reading, it can be said of her, "She . . . worketh willingly with her hands."

Second, these were talented hands.

They were talented in *making beautiful things.* Like the woman in the Scripture who "layeth her hands to the spindle," Cecil Martin excelled in all kinds of sewing and related skills. She made beautiful hand-pieced quilts. She made lovely and intricate crocheted pieces of all types, even up to her 91st year. She made decorative doilies, tablecloths, and bedspreads, including this beautiful bedspread across her casket. In her hands is an unfinished doily.

She made crafts of all kinds. Many people came to her when she was in the nursing home, wanting to purchase her work, and she was able to help buy her medicine and have a little extra herself, thus keeping a sense of independence.

Her hands were *talented in baking.* Many of you will remember the delicious pound cakes and home-made yeast rolls she made from scratch and her delight in sharing them.

Her hands were *talented in music.* She learned music as a child on an old pump organ and played the piano, accordion, Autoharp, and harmonica. She freely used this talent in tent revival meetings, church services, and especially in the nursing home.

There she played for most all the church services and other functions, some 14! She was always willing to use her musical talent for the Lord and to encourage others. As active as she was, I'd be surprised if she's not already playing for the heavenly orchestra.

They were touching hands.

Her daughter, Kathryn, vividly remembers from childhood feeling her mother's hand on her forehead as she checked for fever during long nights of sickness. After all these years she recalls how reassuring that touch felt.

Some of you can remember seeing Mrs. Martin walking home from church in cold weather, spreading her coat over Kathryn and drawing her inside, much as a mother hen covers her chicks with her wings. So Kathryn's mother covered her one chick with her coat, where she felt warm and safe.

She also touched the lives of many others. Long before the phone company coined the phrase "Reach out and touch someone," Cecil Martin was already reaching out to others and continued to do so all her life.

During World War II she made trip after trip to New Orleans, donating blood for our soldiers, giving so much she became ill.

Here in Ponchatoula she wrote a fellow neighbor, Spencer Fendlason, also a pallbearer today, while he was a prisoner of war in Germany. She touched his life thousands of miles away from home by writing cheerful news about his family and community. She checked on his wife, Lillian, and their family and encouraged them in every way she could. One of her most prized possessions is the postal card Spencer mailed to her from Germany in 1945. It will be presented to the Fendlason family after this service.

There is not time to tell all. But she continued to reach out her hands to others even after she went into the nursing home. One example involved a 92-year-old woman who had been very active. But when she began to get depressed, she took to her bed and just gave up. For days, Cecil Martin, already 90 herself, wheeled in to sit by her bed and encourage her. She kept doing this until the older lady got up and resumed her activities of walking, picking up litter in the parking lot, and working in the tiny garden behind the nursing home.

During the Persian Gulf War, Cecil Martin wrote to some 30 soldiers in Saudi Arabia.

She sewed on buttons and mended the clothes of a blind man and other residents in the nursing home who needed help. As the Scripture says, "She reacheth forth her *hands* to the needy" [emphasis added].

She was the "mail lady" for the nursing home, and as she delivered the mail from her wheelchair, she often stopped to visit and encourage the bedridden. She read mail to those who could no longer see and even *wrote* letters for many.

Time forbids telling of any more examples, and only eternity will show the extent of her "touching hands."

Not only were Cecil Martin's hands toiling hands, talented hands, and touching hands, but also

They were trusting hands.

I'm sure we all have seen that famous picture *Praying Hands.* As those hands were clasped in prayer, so too were this lady's hands and heart lifted up to God in trust. She trusted Him for her salvation many, many years ago. And throughout her long life, she trusted Him to take care of her.

She also trusted and loved His Word. Her hands held her precious Bible as she read it every morning.

She quoted the 23rd psalm in the hospital and sang "It's Real." On Friday she told many visiting friends, "I'm ready to go anytime." A few hours later she slipped away to be with Jesus and others awaiting her on the other side, just three hours from her 91st birthday.

So hers were trusting hands.

Conclusion

Many years ago a young mother lay dying. She called her oldest little girl, age 12, and asked her to make three promises:

1. Take care of your little brothers and sisters.
2. Help your drunken father all you can.
3. Try to win others to Jesus.

Maggie promised.

She continued taking in washing as her mother had. She scrubbed on an old rub board until her hands were raw and bleeding. She earned barely enough to feed her brothers and sisters. She tried to help her father.

Then Maggie became very ill. As she was dying, she talked to a friend of her mother. "I tried to keep the promises I made, but I could keep only the first two. What will I tell Jesus when I stand before Him?"

The friend replied, "Don't tell Him anything, Maggie. Just show Him your hands. And when He sees your broken, bleeding hands that you have used for Him, He will say, 'Well done, thou good and faithful servant. . . . Enter thou into the joy of thy lord'" (Matt. 25:21).

And when Cecil Martin stands before Jesus and holds out her hands—her well-worn, toiling hands, her talented hands she used for Him, her touching hands she used to help others, and her trusting hands that reached out to Him—then I believe He will look at her hands and say, "Well done, thou good and faithful servant. . . . Enter thou into the joy of thy lord."

Then when this life of labor is ended,
    And the reward of the race you have run,
Oh! the sweet rest prepared for the faithful
    Will be His blest and final "Well done."

But if you try and fail in your trying,
    Hands sore and scarred from the work you've begun,
Take up your cross; run quickly to meet Him.
    He'll understand; He'll say, "Well done."

Chorus:
Oh, when I come to the end of my journey,
    Weary of life, and the battle is won,
Bearing the staff and the cross of redemption,
    He'll understand, and say, "Well done."

—Lucie E. Campbell

"Give her of the fruit of her hands; and let her own works praise her in the gates" (Prov. 31:31).

To friends and loved ones, I bring you comfort. Jesus said, "I will not leave you comfortless" (John 14:18).

Ordinarily at this point I would address the family. But with Kathryn's being the only child, I will address my remarks to her. Take comfort in them.

Take comfort in the fact that your mother lived a long and productive life.

Take comfort in the fact that you were a good and faithful daughter.

You came here between speaking seasons, visiting her at least once a day and many times twice a day or more. You saw to her needs and took her out whenever she wanted to go. You made her Christmas visits home special.

When your work called you away, you wrote every week and sometimes more often. You sent cards for every occasion, Easter, Valentine's, birthdays . . .

You telephoned every Saturday and other times as well.

It's normal for those who lose a loved one to have some regrets or some guilt. But if there is ever someone who should have *no* regrets, someone who should feel *no* guilt, it's you, Kathryn. So take comfort in that.

And finally take comfort that you will see her again someday. Only you won't be standing over a bed watching her suffer. She will be young and pain-free forever. Take comfort from that.

There's One who can comfort when all else fails,
Jesus, blessed Jesus.
His arm is around when the foe assails,
Jesus, blessed Jesus.
Once He traveled the way we go,
Felt the pangs of deceit and woe;
So who more perfectly, then, can know
Than Jesus, blessed Jesus?

—Charles H. Gabriel

Dear Father, we commend this service into Thy hands. We commend these people into Thy hands.

Oh, what an outpouring of love there has been this day and in the past few days for Cecil Martin and for her

*daughter, Kathryn, to show love and appreciation! What
wonderful people there are here today! We pray Thy abun-
dant blessing upon them.*

*Now may we go from here out to the burial with the
certain knowledge that Jesus is with us and He will not
leave us comfortless.*

*Help us to remember that as Cecil Martin used <u>her</u>
hands for Jesus, may we use <u>our</u> hands for the Lord Jesus
Christ.*

In Thy precious name. Amen.

*   *   *

When everyone had filed past for final viewing en
route to the cemetery, I got up from the seat where I'd been
nestled into one of Mother's afghans.

Leaning over the casket, I whispered, "Mama, I'm going to keep your crocheting you've started, but I'm leaving
you another little ball of thread and a crochet needle. And
I'm leaving your harmonica and your kazoo.

"I'm so very proud of you, Mama. Did you see all
those people who turned out for you? Did you see how
many lives you touched? And there are many more still
calling. And you worried about having stars in your
crown!"

I finished, "Thank you for everything, Mama. I love
you."

For the first time in my life since she'd learned to say
it back, there was no answer.

I placed a good-bye kiss on the thick silver hair and
walked away from my mother, my child.

EPILOGUE

One of the hardest things I had to do was to stop at the nursing home the day after the funeral. I found the hallways and activities areas virtually empty. There was a hush on the entire place.

Many of those usually out and about were seated in their rooms, some even lying in bed. Mother had been so visible and such a part of each individual life that her death made a great impact. She had come back so happy to be home, and they had just expected she would mend, and everything would be the same. Yet when they had awakened the next morning, she was gone. There had been no warning, no chance to say good-bye.

If I had it to do over, I would have asked the nursing home for permission to use a little side room to receive the residents and their visitors, complete with a guest register. Maybe I would even have asked Jacklyn to bring a few words of comfort. For they seemed to be at loose ends and needed to express their good-byes through me, thus giving them something definite.

I popped into a number of rooms, making sure each private treasure had been returned from Mother's safekeeping to its rightful owner. Oh, what welcomes I received! And how many comments on the beautiful funeral they'd already heard about!

"Here's $4.00 that belonged to your mother," one lady said. "My son sold some of her little crosses in his office in Baton Rouge." (Mother had been thrilled about that, for he had taken a bunch of her work and priced it higher than she had, giving the profit to her.)

I thanked our friend and told her I'd put it toward the family spray. She seemed pleased.

Word passed that I was there, and people came out to express sympathy and tell me what Mother had meant to them. Relatives told me that if it hadn't been for her, their loved ones would not have adjusted and recovered a measure of health. Many assured me they'd be watching out for Mr. B.

Even the lady who couldn't talk expressed herself. As I usually do for those in wheelchairs, I knelt on the floor to be eye level and talk to her. She extended her good arm to me, drew me close, and held me as she sobbed silently.

"Please don't forget us," I heard again and again.

"We know it'll be hard on you to come back, but please come whenever you can. We loved your mother, and we love you."

Much as at the funeral home, I was able to tell each one Mother's personal comments concerning them.

I found Mr. B. secured to his wheelchair and, once again, kissed him good-bye. He stared straight ahead from his Alzheimer's world, saying nothing.

I kept my promise about no cancellations and left to begin my winter speaking tour in four days. With my heart unbearably heavy, off I flew to bring laughter and encouragement to others. It was made even more difficult because Jacklyn was having surgery that very morning. She'd learned of her malignancy two days before Mother's death and had postponed the operation to conduct Mother's services. At the time I didn't know she would recover and do well. I just felt I needed to be in two places at one time and wondered if I was to lose both mothers in one week. Only God himself could supply the grace that helped me get through that period.

Within a few weeks Mr. B. rallied to ask, "When is Mrs. Martin coming back?" The nurse gently explained what had happened and asked if he understood. He nodded.

He never spoke again and soon went into a coma. I continued to call the nursing home and the hospital to check on him by long distance. Less than three months after Mother's death, the hospital called to say that he had died. From my hotel I called the funeral home to set a tentative date for the weekend.

In a few minutes, somewhat numb, I went directly to my last speaking engagement of the week. The next morning I flew back to Memphis and drove on to Louisiana.

During the hours of the trip I imagined Mother's surprise upon seeing Mr. B. Often when she'd been out "gallivanting" and Mr. B. awakened from his nap searching for her, she would laugh and welcome him with, "Man, can't I go anywhere without you following me?" And they'd laugh together as he said, "It doesn't look like it!"

I could just hear her "Man, can't I even go to heaven without you following me?" accompanied by their happy laughter and his "It doesn't look like it!" (Of course, it's a good thing there won't be any marrying or giving in marriage in heaven, as I don't know what Daddy would have to say about all this!)

Besides his nursing home stay, Mr. B. had never lived in Ponchatoula, so he had wanted a graveside service only. The Masons made the long drive, but each thought the other was to lead and hadn't brought whatever was needed. So they asked the funeral director to speak. He delivered a wonderfully inspirational sermon. I sat with Mr. B.'s son, much as I'd seen Mother sit with Mr. B. in hard times—with an arm around him and patting his arm as he wept, although we had not met previously.

Then on that beautiful spring day I addressed the son and his children, who had come from across the country, telling them about those last few years—how active, well liked, and respected Mr. B. had been. His roommate's wife and a nursing home representative verified this from their seats in the informal service. I then comforted them with Mr. B.'s testimony of turning his life over to the Lord. I concluded by thanking them for sharing their loved one with my mother, that he had turned her life around—and that if it had been up to the two of them, his dad and my mom, we would be attending this service as "brother" and "sister"!

So on that upbeat note, we laid Mr. B. to rest at Mother's feet. (And, yes, Mama, there are always flowers.)

My book still has no ending, however, with stories of Mother's influence continuing to pour in, whether by mail or phone, on the street, or in the nursing home. So often I hear, "You know, I really enjoyed your mama's funeral— oh, I'm sorry . . . well, I don't know how else to say it—I *did* enjoy it. I'd never heard one like that, and it fit Mrs. Martin so perfectly."

"That's OK," I reassure. "It was meant to be enjoyed. I enjoyed it myself and still derive comfort from it. When I hurt so badly I think I can't stand it, I go over every detail in my mind and get strength to go on."

And go on I do.

I laugh at Mother's wit. I cry from my sorrow. I break up the last of the pecans she bought with her own money and shelled for me as a birthday present and sprinkle them atop my zucchini quiche flavored with "false salt and pepper." I wash my dishes and my minivan with loofahs from her bumper-crop years.

I remember how she depended upon me and needed me. But I also remember the Family Christmas Night that I made a special effort to get there to be with her—and how she had so many outside guests and gifts that, while the band played, I stood in a corner alone, feeling the way we do when our children start school and one day announce, "You don't have to go with me anymore; I'm *big* now."

I swell with a nice pride when I see those she encouraged continue in the paths she steered them. I hear from staff members and others how they went to Mother with their problems and found solace there.

I see her crocheting and her plants in home after home. But I remember her disappointment in not being able to grow a rosa montana.

At the nursing home for a visit, an aide led me out into the little backyard, and we both had goose bumps and tears when she pointed, "See? It's your mama's rosa montana blooming its little head off for her!"

No, it's not over yet.

As Jacklyn said at Mother's interment:

"Let not your heart be troubled: ye believe in God, believe also in me. In my Father's house are many mansions: if it were not so, I would have told you. I go to prepare a place for you. And if I go and prepare a place for you, I will come again, and receive you unto myself; that where I am, there ye may be also" (John 14:1-3).

Now as we come to lay Cecil Martin's body to rest, I hold in this little container the soil from her native Kentucky, which will be sprinkled into her grave.

Over a period of time the Kentucky soil and the Louisiana soil will pack together and become hard. But one day—one day—a trumpet is going to sound. And as that trumpet announces our Lord's return to earth, this hard-packed ground will crack open, and Cecil Martin will burst forth to meet Him in the air. Not the aged, worn body we are burying today, but a new, youthful, glorified body that will never again know sickness or pain or death!

No, it's not over yet! Take comfort in that!